DELIBERATE GROWTH® FOR LEADERS

DkK GROUP MEDIA

DkK Group Media
Kansas City Metro Area

Copyright © 2025 Center for Deliberate Growth®
Published by DkK Group Media

All rights reserved. This book or parts thereof may not be reproduced in any form, stored in any retrieval system, or transmitted in any form by any means—electronic, mechanical, photocopy, recording, or otherwise—without prior written permission of the author or publisher, except as provided by United States of America copyright law. For information regarding permission requests, contact the author at *debrakunz.com*.

ISBNs:
        eBook   979-8-9921166-1-8
        Paperback   979-8-9921166-0-1
Library of Congress Control Number: 2024926242

First Edition
Book Production and Publishing by Brands Through Books
brandsthroughbooks.com

By reading this document, the reader agrees that under no circumstances is the author or the publisher responsible for any losses, direct or indirect, which are incurred as a result of the use of information contained within this document, including, but not limited to, errors, omissions, or inaccuracies.

Legal Notice:
This book is copyright protected. Please note the information contained within this document is for educational and personal use only. You cannot amend, distribute, sell, use, quote or paraphrase any part, or the content within this book, without the consent of the author or publisher.

For information about the author visit *debrakunz.com*.

DELIBERATE GROWTH® FOR LEADERS

DISCOVER BLIND SPOTS, ACTIVATE TEAMWORK,

ACCELERATE RESULTS

DEBRA KUNZ

DkK
GROUP MEDIA

Praise for Deliberate Growth® for Leaders

"This book is an indispensable resource for those leaders who are both looking to set strong pathways for their teams and their own actions as a deliberate leader, or for those experienced leaders who have a sense that they may need a "reset." Debra is a plain-spoken voice who keeps it real!"
—JANA MEYERS, President-Elect, Association for Talent Development, Kansas City

"In *Deliberate Growth® for Leaders*, Debra Kunz provides a compelling and actionable framework for leaders to move beyond reactive management and proactively cultivate intentional, collaborative leadership. Through strategic insights and practical applications, this book empowers leaders to unlock team potential and accelerate innovation. A must-read for leaders committed to creating environments where excellence and transformation thrive."
—JOSÉ PIRES, Founder & CEO, Global Excellence & Innovation

"*Deliberate Growth® for Leaders: Discover Blind Spots, Activate Teamwork, Accelerate Results* is a must read for anyone desiring to step up their leadership game. Debra combines her powerful tools with wit and compelling everyday examples that anyone in a leadership role can relate to and learn from."
—DAWN HAHN, Sr. Laboratory Operations Director (retired), Quest Diagnostics

"Debra Kunz offers leaders a practical framework to overcome stagnation, foster engagement, and drive meaningful growth. This book is a must-read for anyone ready to embrace innovative thinking and lead their teams to achieve exceptional results."
—MEGAN BOZZUTO, President, International Association of Women

"I really enjoyed the practical ways Debra challenges leaders to slow down, be the change, and be curious. Loved the blend of emotional intelligence and the real-life stories to weave her principles into the sticky situations leaders face. If you want to empower versus control your team, this book is for you."

—Dan Stalp, President of Sandler, co-author of the Reunion Trilogy series

"For leaders seeking fresh perspectives and powerful resources, Debra Kunz's *Deliberate Growth® for Leaders* is a must read. Her insights on listening with your heart and soul and mastering the five factors for creating change will revolutionize your leadership and team dynamics. Don't miss this game-changing guide!"

—Carol Weber, Vice President Operations & Customer Care, epay North America, a division of Euronet Worldwide

"Debra Kunz creates a road map for sane, sensible, and successful leadership growth. A must read."

—Rebecca Forster, USA Today Best-Selling Author

"*Deliberate Growth® for Leaders*" is a transformative guide for leaders ready to reflect, grow, and elevate their leadership style. With wit, insight, and a belief in positive change, Debra helps leaders unlock their highest potential. A game changer for those seeking personal and leadership growth."

—Lizzie Foster, Founder & Wellbeing Coach, Wayfarer Yoga and Wellness

"A much needed reminder, in the chaos of growth and expansion, to slow down and be intentional in the leadership of my law firm and to remain connected and "aligned" with my team through more effective communication. I love the concept of intentional curation of positive work environments and will be taking steps to implement some of Debra's very sensible and practical advice."

—SOPHIE STANBROOK, Partner, Stanbrook Prudhoe

"Debra Kunz has an uncanny way of helping leaders and their senior teams see what had been invisible to them, and then create space and direction to make the changes that this new vision prompted. Her book is a gift to any leader who needs some support to 'see' what's missing or what's not obvious. It's written in Deb's voice, which is filled with Deb's wisdom and very serious insights into how to fix challenging organizational problems."

—CAROLE HERSEY BERGERON, PhD, Healthcare Executive (retired)

*For all the leaders who want
to make a difference.*

CONTENTS

Introduction	1
Chapter 1. **Turn Off Autopilot**	11
Chapter 2. **Team Troubles**	23
Chapter 3. **The Challenge of Changing Results**	33
Chapter 4. **Lead Not React**™	43
Chapter 5. **Teamwork Transformed**™	61
Chapter 6. **Recalibrate for Results**™	79
Chapter 7. **Optimize Communication**	93
Chapter 8. **Activate Change**	115
Chapter 9. **The Chain Reaction for Deliberate Growth**®	129
Chapter 10. **The Ripple Effect**	143
Acknowledgments	155

NOTE TO READERS

This publication contains the opinions and ideas of its author. It is intended to provide helpful and informative material on the subjects addressed. The strategies outlined in this book may not be suitable for every individual or organization and are not guaranteed or warranted to provide any particular results.

While the client stories shared in this book are true, some details have been changed to protect their privacy.

INTRODUCTION

During my performance review, I handed my boss my review of the company. This was the first time I reviewed a business. And it was right after college when I was working for this small startup business in tech, about thirty years ago.

My boss was based in another city, so working remotely in a hybrid situation was familiar to me. Fortunately, we were in the same room for this conversation. After we were finished with my review, I boldly spoke up to say that I had developed a summary of my observations about the business. My breathing quickened a little, though I was surprisingly calm. The quizzical look on his face left me wondering if he was open to this idea.

Did I mention that he didn't ask me to review how the company functioned? Of course, I wouldn't have done it without having built a relationship with him where I thought he would listen. And he did listen.

He read the entire report. I talked about the company culture where people were viewed as cogs in the system, not as essential, and definitely not as human. I also talked about how each person was valuable and their expertise contributed to the overall goal of the business, but we never addressed or discussed that in the company. The staff meetings were entirely project- and task-completion-driven. There was never time for questions, and they were always led with the assumption by the leaders that everyone knew what they were talking about. We didn't. I mentioned the burnout among the developers, the lack of trust and collaboration across the company, the rising cost of rework and risk to deadlines, and the building of combative dynamics between employees. There was a general lack of productivity despite having a stocked kitchen that kept people at work at all hours.

Know what my boss did after he read the report? When I ask my speaking audiences that question, someone usually yells, "You got fired!" Thankfully, I didn't.

He said with a heavy sigh, "You're absolutely right. And it will never change." My mouth dropped open at the thought that he knew about all of these leadership problems at the company, and that he wasn't going to do anything about them. Then I sighed with a deep exhale as I realized that he was being very frank with me about whether he believed the ownership group would do anything about solving them.

I was speechless, and for this extrovert, that takes a lot. Running through my head were thoughts like, "Seriously??? How could you possibly lead a business with this toxic environment that dismisses people's value and be okay with that? I just outlined what it's costing the people and the business as a result." Wow. Just wow!

Later, I was replaying in my head what he had said, still in disbelief that he really wasn't going to do anything about it. Nothing. Zero. Nada. He was serious that nothing would ever change, even though I was right about everything.

So . . . I made the change because that wasn't a situation that I was going to be able to influence enough to want to stay. The leaders weren't interested in any other viewpoints or how changing the way they lead could actually get them to their goals on time—and maybe *faster*. There was a total lack of interest in developing people, not to mention the leaders developing themselves. As I read through my original report, this observation of a small business was the beginning of my passion for building better leaders as an executive coach.

I moved to a large corporation, thinking that a bigger company with more resources would have better leaders and invest in developing their leaders. And that the environment would be less paternal and more aligned with understanding the importance of the people who were essential to delivering on the services the company provided. I hoped that my contribution would be understood and valued, and the leaders would care about the gifts, strengths, and attributes that I brought to the company.

Nothing was different in working with the leaders at the bigger company. It was just more complicated, given there were larger numbers of employees involved in a more difficult business structure. Growth in a business starts with its leaders, and up until this point in my career, I found many leaders weren't interested in prioritizing how to grow themselves.

In fact, during a ten-year period, I navigated ten mergers. Some were internal ownership changes, which means who I worked for changed—again. Some changes were client-facing, and at one point, there were three brand changes in three years. The clients didn't even know who we were at that point; they would just call and ask for Joe. If Joe still worked there, Joe knew what that client needed, even if the surrounding company had no clue.

The daily chaos created by the constantly changing priorities made me shake my head so often that I had to see a chiropractor. Picture the face-palm emoji. An ambivalent culture developed a "whatever" attitude that focused on "as long as my direct deposit came through, I don't care which name is on it this week."

With an exasperated exhale, I shrugged my shoulders, but it drove me nuts that no one really knew what was going on on any given day. Why didn't they know? Because the grapevine was the communication avenue, and if you've ever played a game of telephone, you know it's not reliable. The formal meeting structure only told us the watered-down version of information, not what we needed to make decisions on projects every day. So, we had to rely on other avenues to find out what we needed to do our jobs.

It was mind-numbing how much time this consumed! And how it drained my energy and used time that could have been spent on other projects. And it was entirely preventable if the leaders knew how to lead! Not just for my sake—for everyone's sake, including the leaders themselves.

It became clear that when I led a project, I had different expectations of how people were to work together. It wasn't always met with excitement. There was usually resistance to changing how things were done, which I always found ironic given people didn't like how things were done, but didn't want to change either. Often, people scowled at the notion of meeting more often, not less, and having more expectations of being prepared, not less. I would get that head-cocked-to-the-side, crossed-arms-with-an-icy-glare look.

I just smiled and warmly reviewed the next steps because I knew what they didn't—their jobs and their lives were about to get easier. They just didn't know that yet. So, I invited them to try doing things differently, and I **showed them** during the meetings how everyone actually had the same goal: to produce quality work on time.

What happened? One by one, the representatives from each functional area would come to me and thank me for being tenacious. For not allowing the status quo to win again. For guiding them to find their voice. For helping them see that talking with each other leads to better solutions for the customer and faster resolutions for them.

We spent less time on rework because we figured things out ahead of time. As a result, I essentially became an internal consultant. I would be requested by the functional business areas because "projects just worked better" when I led them. Execs would ask me to lead internal projects required by the latest buyout or merger. They would drop the initiative in my lap and know that I would "figure it out." Which I did. I was also being asked to mentor other leaders and to share insights into leading teams and communication issues like "How on earth do you get people to talk with each other?"

It showed a level of trust in my leadership and my tenacity in producing quality outcomes. What they might not have realized was that **how** I worked with the team was vastly different from how I observed others doing it. It's why I created the *Pivotal Principles for Leading Deliberate Growth®*.

During that decade of breath-holding and will-I-have-a-job-tomorrow changes, I was retained every time, and earned an MBA. For every ownership change, there was a risk of consolidating staff and layoffs. Each time, my name must have been on the list since I wasn't a billable resource. I was a business brain who could lead teams through project plans that I invented from scratch. My strategic thinking and communication skills were a unique strength. My understanding of how to value each person and facilitate ideas and discussions meant I could get people from across the organization to talk with each other.

In all of these companies, big and small, the leaders didn't take time to **value** the people who worked at the business, although all would be offended by that notion. Why? Because it's a *massive blind spot*. Many knew they were "the boss," though few knew how **to lead**.

None of these leaders intended to be dismissive of their teams. None of these leaders intended to create an environment where teamwork was an afterthought, assuming it was something that people "just did."

These leaders from all sizes of companies were hyper-focused on creating business results, managing costs, and delivering to deadlines. That's not wrong. The problem was that they forgot that doing all those things required all of their teams to be producing at peak performance. And that each individual needed the correct information to make the best decisions about their own contributions. And that each person needed to be treated as a human before being treated as an employee.

When chaos becomes your normal, you sometimes forget that a more peaceful life is possible. I like to be busy but not frantic. I like adventure and challenges but not constant uncertainty. I realized that I wanted to be able to see the impact of the effort and energy I was contributing through my profession.

So, I left my corporate role to do something more entrepreneurial where I could see the impact I was having on people, and contribute to their lives. I spent six years in the financial industry using my fearless nature of asking meaningful questions and my gift for strategic thinking to help professionals and business owners plan and invest for their financial futures.

I loved the education I'd received in money management and the hours I'd spent studying for licensing exams. It's so much fun to teach people about their options with money and how to connect them to their life and business goals.

Clients kept asking me business questions, sometimes more often than investing questions. They knew about my experience with complex business scenarios—hello, ten mergers in ten years! They were asking about cultivating teamwork or how to handle a difficult business decision or what they could be doing better as a leader.

I realized that my passion for solving business problems by building better leaders far outweighed my desire to answer questions about the stock market. In 2010, I founded my executive coaching and leadership development business that was later named the Center for Deliberate Growth®.

How you lead directly affects the results you create. Watching the miscommunication and misunderstandings between leaders and teammates and seeing the impact on the business was mind-boggling.

Having it be continuously dismissed as "nothing," as it clearly frustrated all the people involved, was exasperating, especially for those who had to redo their work as a result. Miscommunication complicates scheduling, drains people of their energy, compresses deadlines for other projects, puts product or system projects at risk, and creates doubt in your clients/customers.

It's an entirely preventable cost!!!

Building confidence and self-awareness in leaders always makes for better business results. In fact, I've found that building these qualities in all employees magnifies those results. We are each responsible for leading ourselves, even if we don't have a team of people who report to us.

Introduction

What happens when we build better leaders? People speak up with questions. And they answer questions without taking them personally. They dare to challenge the status quo. They engage in teamwork without concerns about the backlash of conflict. Problem-solving becomes more thorough and efficient. Information flow shifts from restricting it and worrying about who knows what to an understanding of who **needs** to know what and sharing it accordingly. The team focuses on the goals of the business, not just their own, because they understand how their contribution fits into that bigger picture.

In my experience coaching executive leaders, they feel a deep sense of relief when they finally have an ally who tells them the absolute truth. Maybe you're lucky enough to have a collaborative business partner or a peer group in the company that gives it to you straight. It's crucial to have an expert to learn from, bounce ideas off, and examine situations or explore opportunities with.

My purpose with this book is to teach you transformational principles that will help you get out of your own way. I'm here to help you reignite your leadership spark so that you can quickly grow the business with an engaged team beside you. To achieve this, you must shift how you think about yourself as a leader.

You're reading the right book if . . .

- You feel like you've plateaued as a leader and realize that how you've been leading isn't working, but you don't know what to change to make it better.
- You're preparing for rapid growth and want to prevent people problems before they happen so that you can go on vacation without checking in.
- You're experienced, and you feel like you should already know how to do this "leadership stuff," but you don't, and it feels like you're behind.

- Your leadership team is working in silos instead of together. This typically means that your other teams are too.
- You want to grow yourself and quickly develop the leaders in your succession plan.
- You know you're doing too much of the work yourself, but can't seem to change the pattern you're in.
- You just took over or inherited teams that you didn't hire and need to get your arms around their dynamics.
- You feel overwhelmed, have lost your nerve, and wonder if there's a way you could cope with setbacks in a healthy, productive way instead of stewing about them for days on end.
- You want to develop more confidence in yourself as a leader who can navigate conflict and create the growth you seek for yourself, your team, and the business.

Use this book as your coach for today. Read the book from start to finish—without assumptions. If you want to grow as a leader, don't jump to conclusions that you "already know this" or "already heard about that." There is a big difference between intellectually knowing something and actually applying it effectively.

Throughout this book, you'll find key insights at the start of each chapter. These are reflections I've shared with clients during pivotal moments, offering guidance and clarity in their journeys. They work as key insights to keep in mind for each chapter.

As I compiled all my experience from the last three decades with companies small to large and in a variety of industries, my *5 Pivotal Growth Principles* emerged. Each principle will move you to become a better leader and make it easier to create the results you want. Together, these transformational leadership elements will create *Deliberate Growth*® in you, your team, and your business.

INTRODUCTION

The 5 Pivotal Principles for Leading Deliberate Growth®

1. Lead Not React™
2. Teamwork Transformed™
3. Recalibrate for Results™
4. Optimize Communication
5. Activate Change

The key is to understand these transformational growth principles and **apply** them to how you lead. Intellectually understanding them doesn't create change in yourself, your team, or the business. It's only when they change how you think about things that your behavior changes, your performance shifts, and your results accelerate.

There's a chapter for each *Pivotal Growth Principle*, illustrated by my client stories and examples. I also cover leadership blind spots that prevent growth, sticky situations leaders face, and how to navigate conflict.

We spend the majority of our time at work. My mission is to build better leaders who create environments where everyone thrives, including the leader. These environments should be composed of people who empower us, develop us, and expand our potential, all while creating great business results. I choose to focus on leaders because of their influence on the lives of others.

I'm known for my down-to-earth thinking, practical wisdom, warm wit, and candidness. I'm also known for being insightful and intuitive; I quickly get to the heart of the matter instead of talking around the issue.

I'm so happy you're here to learn and grow. Let's get started!

CHAPTER 1

TURN OFF AUTOPILOT

The first step is getting out of your own way.

Have you ever tried applying what you've learned, but it doesn't work out the way you thought it would? Your intentions are good. You know the team you want to build. You know the environment you want to create for yourself and for your teams to thrive in. But it isn't happening like that.

Or maybe things in the company are a big mess, and you're not sure where to begin. Perhaps the frustration has taken over as you feel the energy drain from you each day. Something has got to give. You can't keep working like this.

You've now discovered that "lonely at the top" isn't just a saying. It's a reality. Leaders, there's nothing wrong with needing help and support for yourself. There's no award for leading the business all by yourself. In fact, trying to do it yourself might cost you growth because you're spinning your wheels instead of getting out of your own way.

Or maybe things are going okay, and you want to make them better, but you don't know what you don't know, and you want someone to light the path for you.

If you're asking yourself, *What do I need to change as the leader to take the business to the next level?* you're in the right place. What "next level" means is entirely up to you. This could mean:

- More revenue
- Better margins
- Introducing a new product or service
- Branching out to a new client/customer base

- Higher customer/client satisfaction levels
- Meeting service levels or production quality standards
- Hiring more people
- Streamlining internal operations
- Raising employee retention
- Creating an engaged learning and growth culture

After more than fifteen years of coaching executive leaders, business owners, and entrepreneurs, and a prior seventeen-year corporate career, I've found that leaders can't run the business by themselves. Yet, as the leader, you might feel like you're alone with the pressure of growth squarely on your shoulders. And only on your shoulders. Not true. Read on.

As the leader, you are responsible for setting the tone. For creating, building, and engaging the team. For generating the business results. Your ability to lead has an exponential impact on how your team performs and the business results that are created. And yet, it's not just about you.

It starts with you. But it's not only about you. We'll talk more about that in later chapters as I guide you through my *5 Pivotal Principles for Leading Deliberate Growth®*. These transformational leadership elements are cumulative, so be sure to read the chapters in order, without making assumptions about what you do or don't already know, to truly leverage your learning.

For now, let's focus on how you might be feeling about the business at the moment. Which of these are going on right now? Or is it something else?

- You want to grow but don't know what to do differently.
- You're frustrated with your team and maybe with yourself.
- Your business performance has plateaued or is sliding backward.

- You want to learn more about how to be a better leader because you're unaware of your leadership style and its impact on others.
- Your team asks you for answers instead of figuring it out for themselves.
- Big changes are on the horizon, and you want to prevent problems.
- Priorities are addressed, though not in the order you thought you conveyed.
- People aren't speaking up even though you invite them to and genuinely want them to share their ideas. Or the opposite—everyone talks, but nobody listens.
- You're not sure how to begin.

The first step to developing a solution is to understand where you are starting from.

What's Getting in the Way?

Stop operating on autopilot. Another way to think about it is leading by default aka the mode of operation you always use every day. It might not even be conscious yet. That's one of the reasons you're here reading this book—to learn more about yourself and how you function as a leader.

One autopilot mode of operation could be that because your to-do list is never-ending, you're always focused on "just getting something done." Understandable, except just getting things done generally means you're merely focused on completing something, not necessarily a thorough exploration of that item. And that's the example you're setting for your team. No, I'm not suggesting that you seek perfection. That's not a focus that's productive for anyone either.

I'm saying that leading in a rush means you probably jump to conclusions instead of pausing to ask for clarification. In your head, you think you're saving time by "just getting on with it" and "not bothering anyone else with the questions," or you think "those details don't matter anyway."

The truth is this is costing you time and results. How often do you find yourself thinking, "That's not what I meant?" Perhaps your team has used the same "rush to get things done" mentality, and they didn't do what you wanted, or they missed a very important detail.

Blindly leading on autopilot is causing mistakes.

Here's the cost: lots of rework! The reason is usually stated as "that was just a misunderstanding"—like it's okay that those happen ten times per week or per day! It costs thousands of dollars every week in rework or delays—and puts deadlines and client/customer relationships at risk.

Now, it's okay to be a human and make mistakes. What I'm saying is **slow down**. Stop leading by default in a hurry to get stuff done. If this sounds familiar, take a breath. I'll share more about what to correct for yourself, your team, and the business throughout this book.

What Are You Actually Completing?

Another issue with leading on autopilot, and operating by default, is focusing on completion. In your rush, you may have a tendency to work on the "easiest" things first. You could be checking a lot off your list this way, but are those items really the highest priority? Do they have the most impact on moving the business forward? Do they provide the information your team needs so that they can get their work done?

At first glance, this lesson seems like it's about time management, where you are selectively choosing what to complete, but it's not. It's about resisting the urge to lead by default just because you want to feel like you've accomplished something. I get it. I have those days myself. Be careful not to string them together, or you'll wake up a month later, and you've missed all the most impactful high-priority items you actually needed done. Oops.

This behavior also affects how your team operates. Consider how you would react if they were to address their work with a hasty attitude. What if your team focused on what might appear to be the easiest item on their list this week instead of the most important? Or they "finished" something without asking for clarification, and that caused *you* to have to rework everything? Uh-oh.

On the other end of the spectrum, if your version of autopilot means slowing decisions down more than necessary and your projects are delayed, you are putting completion at risk. When this occurs, your teams are waiting on you to make up your mind, so productivity dips.

If this feels familiar, and you're beginning to see yourself, take that as a good thing. It means you know where you are starting from right now.

Mental Focus

Instead of focusing on the project at hand, you're sorta focused on what you're doing while thinking about the next two things you're going to knock off the list, am I right?

In the meantime, your assistant or VP or director or employee just gave you an update on a key project, which you kinda listened to, though not completely. Or you skimmed that email but didn't really read it. This leads to promises made—by you—that you don't necessarily remember. Unfortunately, you create a lot of unkept promises this way. Because how can you keep a promise you don't know you made? Yikes. Stop the madness!

What causes this? It could be:

- The mental exhaustion caused by frequently changing priorities.
- Something at home that has you distracted.
- That you have to collaborate with a colleague you aren't getting along with all that well on a project you're supposed to be prioritizing.

- You haven't taken the time to think through what the project actually requires, so you don't know where to begin.

The first two—mental exhaustion and distractions at home—are an issue with you. The last two, a difficult colleague and not taking time to think through a project, are also an issue with you, the leader, even though they sound like they are about other things.

What do I mean? It's easy to think that avoiding a difficult colleague is about them. If they were easier to work with, things would get done faster, right? But you're the one doing the avoiding—at the expense of the project or initiative or task or whatever you're working on that involves them. I'm not saying they aren't contributing to the situation. They are. They may be difficult to deal with; however, you are the person who has the power to change the interaction with them so that work becomes easier between you, and you avoid each other less. That means work actually gets done faster, with less stress, and your team isn't waiting on you for answers from this person.

The other example, taking time to think through a project, is one that I've seen many times, especially in highly analytical leaders. It's easy to get into the weeds on the mechanics of a project and forget to pull back and look at the whole picture. So, if you are leading in a rush, you jump to conclusions based on the details you assume are true without taking the entire business scenario into consideration. The longer you wait to put on a strategic thinking hat, the more risk you put into creating a lot of rework—for yourself, for your team, and for other teams in the business.

On the flip side, if you are a strategic thinker already but haven't made time to think through the new initiative, the risk to the business is the same. The longer you wait to make investing that time a priority, the more likely you will create rework. Especially if you've conveyed what you know up until now and set expectations with deadlines. Especially since they don't know that you haven't thought it all the way through, and they are taking action based on the information they've been given so far.

If you wait until absolutely everything has been determined, nothing will ever get started. I get that. What I'm talking about is what happens when these decisions are made in a rush and the resulting gap in communication it creates among the people who are implementing that decision—and *making their own decisions* in the process of doing their work.

The mental exhaustion that comes from changing priorities is, in part, created by you, the executive leader. When you are leading in a rush, it's easy to grab new ideas as new solutions. But you aren't thinking through those ideas to evaluate if they actually apply to the goals you stated. So, ask yourself, do you have clear goals for the business? If not, that might be why there are so many changing priorities—because you aren't clear on what you actually want to accomplish yet. (More on aligning priorities, people, and profit in a later chapter.)

When it comes to the distractions at home issue I mentioned above—that's a truth for all of us. We all have lives outside of work that are important to us. It's a very human thing to have stuff going on at home that consumes some time during the workday. We like to think that we focus on work all day, though we know we don't 100 percent of the time. No one does. It's far more acceptable to bring your life to work now than it was at the beginning of my career in the early nineties. Still . . . as the leader, you set the tone for productivity. If you find yourself distracted by something at home, show that you can navigate it and still get work done; it sets an example for your team to follow. You can be a vulnerable human and still be productive at work. And so can your teams.

Everyone Makes Decisions

A surprising way you're getting in your own way is assuming that you're the only decision-maker. I already spoke to this issue a little bit. We often call executive leaders "decision-makers" because of their positional authority and responsibility in the company. Of course, that's true.

What is also true is <u>all</u> of your employees are also decision-makers.

They just have different levels of authority, responsibility, and access to information than you do. And they are making decisions every day, with every email, text, DM, meeting, phone call, or video meeting—each time they prioritize something—or not.

The question I'm constantly asking my clients is, "What are those decisions based on?"

Here we are, back at the issue of leading on autopilot and prioritizing efficiency of your time over everything else. If your default mode of operation is to use less time, you might tend to skip conversations, for example, and your teams are missing information they need to make sound choices to complete the priority projects that directly impact business goals.

Now, imagine duplicating this issue every week or even every day. Operating this way means the results suffer, the people suffer, and growth suffers. Rework soars. Frustration builds. Key people resign. All the while, you think you're being helpful by just trying to consume less time, yours and your team's. But that's not what ends up happening.

For example, one of my small business clients has been creating a succession plan for his retirement. (If your company is a different size, pay less attention to the size and type of business and more attention to the leadership lessons. I know the industry and size of the company affect the complexity of the problems and opportunities. To maximize your learning as you read, focus on the leadership lessons.) This business owner and I have been working together for many years. I've coached him one-on-one, developed the organizational structure necessary for this business to function more effectively, and coached the leaders who became his managers and then were promoted to be the directors. They are now on track to become owners. On the road of this possibility, we needed to develop these emerging leaders into executive-level thinkers.

The owner of this service business with forty-five employees shared that he would have otherwise "winged it" because he didn't know what he didn't know. Working with me kept him more accountable, and "saved" him a few times when it came to employee relations. He could see the value in having a clear plan for communicating the changes. As you continue to read this book, you'll see how the *Pivotal Growth Principles* build on each other and create the experience he described.

This owner is definitely an efficiency thinker. No more meetings than we need. Well, no one wants more meetings than we need, but this wasn't necessarily what needed to be changed. The key to developing these directors to become owners was to change how they communicated with each other and with the existing owner. I'm quite sure that my recommendation of adding another meeting to the schedule made his mind melt a little. It directly conflicts with his efficiency thinking as he was leading on autopilot. He said it would consume time—"waste it," even. Um, not the case.

Despite his objections, he does listen to my guidance and has started having weekly meetings with these two directors. Suddenly, I'm a genius. Why? Because as I taught him, this meeting provides a funnel for the information. For example, he stopped receiving multiple emails from both directors each week unless it was about a burning issue or a specific project. All the one-off questions and status updates were funneled into this weekly conversation. This weekly meeting automatically creates one place where the three of them can discuss current and upcoming projects, and collaborate on new ideas.

What he's learned is that it has built more efficiency, not less, because now they are on the same page and have an avenue to help them remain there. Decisions are now made with real-time information instead of assumptions. This business owner told me he saved a net of two hours a week by adding this meeting to his schedule.

What's Your Blind Spot?

You may have some self-awareness, but we all have blind spots. Those things that we don't know, we don't know. And unless you have a trusted coach or advisor who will mirror back your blind spots with respect to how you lead, you will continue to lead in the dark. Knowing your blind spots is not about changing who you are. It's about building yourself into a better leader.

A common blind spot is caused by the assumption that others think like we do. We humans think that others know what we mean because if someone spoke to us that way, we'd know what they meant. Except . . . others aren't us. They don't have the same background, experiences, or view of life as we do. So, interacting with them in the same way that we would interact with ourselves creates an obstacle in the communication. We are *actively creating confusion* when we are operating from this assumption.

For example, one executive leader, who is also the owner of the company, was nervous about asking direct questions. When he was trying to formulate the "perfect question," he was thinking about it in terms of *his* understanding of the question and how he would respond—not the other person—and not taking into account *their* understanding of the subject matter at hand.

If you've been in the business a while, or you own the company, you may have forgotten what it's like to be early in your career or what it's like to be a middle-level manager—or even a director or VP. Take some time to consider *who* you are talking with each time you have an interaction. That includes groups as well. You don't need to know every detail of each person. You do need to consider that they are not you. Stop assuming what works in communicating with you is what will work for them.

Recognize that we are each different from each other as humans. The person you're talking with and listening to has their own lens of experience that's different from yours. Stop assuming they understand what you mean. Ask them if they do.

Pause for a moment and consider: Are you leading on autopilot?

Symptoms of a Leader on Autopilot

When you ask a question, are you waiting for the other person to answer, or are you uncomfortable in the silence? If the silence bugs you, most likely, you are answering your own question. You might be talking too much and not listening enough. They don't need to say anything because you are going to tell them the answer. See how that creates a loop where they don't speak up?

Here's some direct coaching: Stop being afraid to lead. If your employees intimidate you, this is not about them. This is about your confidence and comfort in being the boss—and in not being liked from time to time.

Another thing to stop is acting like you "know everything" when you really haven't kept up with your email enough to know what's going on. It's better to be honest or figure out how to have someone else know what's happening so that you can stay in the loop without having to read 100 emails per day.

Take a second to consider if you are micromanaging people. Are there people you feel you always have to "be on top of?" It might be an issue with their motivation and performance. The reality check is that it could also be a sign of your need to control things and ensure things are done "your way." The need to stay on top of people could also be a sign that they lack some job knowledge and need more training.

What About the Company Vision?

When was the last time you shared the vision for the business? When have you discussed that as a team? Have you established shared agreements within your team? One of the mistakes I see leaders making is assuming everyone knows the vision of the business because you shared it once years ago—or even a few months ago. The blind spot here is not seeing that *you live in the vision of the business* every day. Your *teams live in the vision of the project* they are working on every day. Yes, the project most definitely should connect to the vision of the business, though it's not likely that your teams can articulate the vision of the business as succinctly as you can. Again, they don't live in it.

Yes, this needs to be addressed. Not so they can parrot you in conveying the vision of the business. ***It's so they can understand how their role fits into it and invest in creating the results that lead to the vision.***

As the executive leader, do not underestimate the need for you to continue to convey the mission and vision of the business, even if you already have a culture where your teams understand and embrace it. People are always more comfortable when there's continued confirmation of what they think they understand. It shows they are still "in the know" and makes them feel relevant. Your high-performing employees want to feel relevant and like they contribute each day.

Because you can't run the business by yourself, successfully working through others is an essential ability of an effective leader. In the next chapter, we'll uncover the troubles in teamwork.

CHAPTER 2

TEAM TROUBLES

Many team issues are preventable when you know what to look for.

Since we are putting humans in a group together, it inevitably leads to some complications. Humans have different personalities, backgrounds, experiences, knowledge, and modes of operation. Team troubles can range from some mild friction caused by a difference of opinion to deep conflict where people are taking things personally. Many issues are preventable when you know what to look for.

Complex Interactive Dynamics

One of the big issues is silence in team meetings. Yes, everyone may be doing their jobs well. That could be true. But if they don't speak up in team meetings, something is going on in that dynamic. It could be because you are doing all the talking and need to talk less and listen more. Or there could be an undercurrent that there's no safety in speaking one's mind, so they just don't say anything. I hate to say it, but if this is the case, instead of listening, they are making their grocery lists, DMing among themselves, or just wishing the meeting would end. Virtual or in person, people can mentally check out.

Watch for the signs. A few include little eye contact, looking at anything except each other or the screen if you are virtual, talking or texting someone who isn't in the meeting—maybe even texting someone who is in the meeting—eye-rolling, grumbling without speaking, blank stares, and a disengaged energy. Another one is if you do ask them a question, they don't have a thoughtful answer because they weren't thinking about the subject of the meeting.

A potential cause of their silence could be that you hold team meetings just because you're supposed to, but aren't invested in the process or the purpose. You show up with stuff to say and ask them to share what's on their mind, but they don't, so you just give up and move on to the next thing. Or you cancel the meetings because you can't think of any updates to share, forgetting that this should be a two-way interaction.

Or the opposite may be true. Everyone is talking, but no one is listening. If your team meetings are energetic and loud, and there's lots of conversation, it shows everyone is willing to engage and speak up. That's the good part. The trouble comes when you get to the end of the meeting, you're out of time, and everyone bolts. People who are always talking probably aren't listening because they are focused on sharing their own ideas and not listening to others.

When people scatter down the hall or suddenly disappear from the virtual screen, there's no conclusion to the discussion. There's no synthesis of the ideas. There have been no decisions made about next steps, which means people leave that conversation thinking different things and drawing different conclusions. Then, they take action based on those assumptions, which might be the opposite of the goals or not in the right priority order. Yes, you can say you'll send a summary email, and everyone will nod about that. But we know that not everyone will read the email. *And even if they do, they are still reading it through the lens of their own conclusions, looking for evidence to back up the actions they are already taking.*

I can feel the waste of time coming from the inevitable rework that was just created. This issue is about learning to lead and facilitate the meeting or having someone assigned to do that each week. Invest in developing the skills they—and you—need to be effective.

Another complaint I hear from teams is one person is dominant. When there are questions that are asked, it's this person who answers them. What people may not realize is that this person is just trying to get others to talk; they just aren't going about it in an effective way. Their intention is to answer the boss's question and engage their teammates. The boss is wishing someone else would talk, but doesn't know how to gently have the dominant person talk less and invite others to talk more.

For one client, this leader was dealing with a very passionate and knowledgeable team member. Those attributes are good—except when he was the person who answered every question, shared an opinion about every idea, and threw in ideas about unrelated items. He consumed so much time during the team meetings that there was no room for others to talk.

Part of being the leader is being able to coach people through these types of blind spots. He wasn't intentionally being overbearing. It was a massive blind spot in how he functioned based on a foundation of insecurity. This caused issues in the team. People didn't want to deal with him. Yes, this sounds like an issue with him. It is, that's true. Except *you* are the leader. It is a leader's role to solve this issue and create a team dynamic where everyone has a voice. There are multiple avenues to solving this issue discussed in this book. You'll see them as you continue to read.

Change and Trust

Things will always be evolving in a business. Change is continuous. The degree of change and impact of change depends upon the business, industry, and goals of the company. How does your team react to changes? How do they react to the unexpected? Do they pull together, or do they go elsewhere for advice and guidance?

What they do is an indication of trust within the team. Without trust, there's no safety for people to seek answers and guidance from their teammates. People won't talk to each other. Instead, they go talk with people they do trust. Except the people they are talking with aren't part of the project you're working on.

How your team behaves when faced with disruption, changing priorities, or competing priorities is a big indicator of the degree of trust, resilience, and adaptability within the team—three key ingredients for high performance. The lack of these characteristics can be both causes and outcomes of performance issues.

Conflict and Differing Viewpoints

Humans are humans. When we get into a group, we are going to disagree about things. Even in the best company cultures, we are going to disagree. In fact, the best company cultures would encourage people to have different viewpoints because it's what sparks innovation. If we all think the same way, then we may agree on a lot, but we aren't forced to explore new things the same way we are when we work with people who have differing perspectives. Digging into a problem or opportunity with a colleague who approaches situations differently than we do automatically provides an opportunity to advance our thinking as we consider a different viewpoint.

Still, our differences can create friction. Your idea is different from her idea and his idea. Or your solution to that problem is different from the other ideas in the room. Or what you believe to be the problem is entirely different from what others believe the problem to be. What happens in your team when you have conflicting approaches to problems? What happens when there's an innovative idea presented that will change things? What does your team do?

If they pull together and communicate more, they are more likely to be functioning in collaboration. If they go outside the team for counsel and advice, they are not. As I already mentioned, going outside the team first is evidence of very little trust within the team. This is an indication that during meetings, everyone just nods in agreement and then spends the next couple hours after the meeting privately talking about all the things that are wrong, or even right, about what was discussed in the meeting.

Huge waste of time right here. Productivity dies when this is how teams function.

It's okay to go outside your team for ideas and guidance *after* you've first worked within the team. When teams do it beforehand, the team is not a team. It's a group of people who are assigned to the same leader. We'll get into what to talk about that builds teamwork and trust later in this book.

Team Leadership Mistakes

If you have taught your teams how to navigate conflict and differing ideas, you do want them to work on figuring out solutions without your intervention. But there comes a time when stepping in with the energy of "we're in this together" can break the ice and solve the situation quickly. Learning the right timing for that takes practice and a willingness for things to get a little messy during the process. Just don't leave the situation messy. It needs a resolution, even if there needs to be a break from the conversation to get there.

Be wary of assuming that your best employees don't need any attention from you. Often, I see leaders at all levels investing a majority of their time in their lowest performers. If they are new employees and are just learning the ropes, that makes sense. If they are struggling to do their job, first examine whether they are getting the right training. Don't assume they are—find out. Depending upon the size of the business, you can ask the employee and their manager directly. If you have multiple layers of leaders, you already know this will cause a lot of commotion, so be prudent in how you approach the quest for information. If you start asking these questions, you may uncover a need to put a higher priority on providing training in the organization.

Be sure to stand up for your team's ideas and needs around your other executives and leaders. Your team will feel important and valued and that you have their back.

Even when you own the company or are in the C-Suite it's important to continue to make business cases for your arguments. It shows your teams how you want to be approached, with thorough and thoughtful information that connects to the goals and produces desired results.

In your role, be careful not to become a mediator (or even a babysitter). Your role is to lead, not to get A to talk to B and listen to them complain about what the other one is or isn't doing. When a leader chooses to focus on keeping peace instead of achieving goals, they stop leading. It's where all the parental analogies of leadership emerge because it's a lot more like running a middle school at that point. Ick.

What you might think are issues with personality or performance might actually be a gap in knowledge. I call it a training gap. The person is frustrated or stressed. You assume they are difficult and it's "how they are" or "their personality." It could very well be. Or it could be that they need knowledge they don't have to do their job, and, for some reason, they don't feel safe to speak up and say they don't know how to do something. Or they don't know what they don't know, so they don't know to ask. Or they don't ask because they don't want to appear stupid, or they think they are supposed to understand everything based on the training that has been provided.

This tells me there's no room in the culture to question things—to question a method, question a leader, or question how they are being taught. While you are the leader, I know that is not what you intended. As with most issues, if that is the truth of the matter, it's better to know than not know, and learn how to recreate the environment and team dynamics to change it.

Causes of Team Troubles

Every person depends upon someone else to do their job. Every. Single. Person. When the company is organized into teams, the people in the team are dependent upon each other, and the teams are dependent upon each other. Team troubles come when each person isn't aware of the fact that others depend on them. Often, we know that we depend on someone else because our frustration is caused by waiting on them to do something. Except, we forget that someone is also waiting on us unless the person we're waiting on is causing us to miss our deadline with the person waiting on us. Yikes! Did you follow that circle?

The work flows through the business. Whatever industry you are in, each team contributes something that is used by another team in some way. When the priorities aren't clear, or the reasons for the priorities aren't clear, the team struggles to know which items to work on first and which ones to work on next. Competing priorities are "normal" for a business to have, though if your teams are confused about which competing priority is actually the priority, they will go in circles or just stop and wait for the new direction to be revealed by you.

Regular company meetings are the place where the executive leaders share updates on how the business is performing and the vision for what's next. It is a consistent opportunity to keep your teams informed and up to date on the business knowledge they need to make decisions about their work every day. Busy, overscheduled leaders cancel these meetings because "people have too much to do already to sit in a meeting." That's a mistake. If this is you, learn how to turn these regular opportunities into an advantage. You might recall my business owner client who scoffed at the idea of adding a director meeting to his schedule every week and then did it anyway at my recommendation. It saved him a net of two hours a week. What could you do with two more hours per week?

You, as the leader, often focus on the productivity of your own team. It's definitely the best place to start, but don't stop there. Every team is dependent upon another team. If your team is performing well, the next biggest risk to productivity is the handoffs between teams.

The performance issues of some team members not delivering on their responsibilities cause stress for the entire team. Someone has to "pick up the slack," and it's usually the same people. This raises the stress of the entire team. What's worse is the team sees the "slacker" get away with doing nothing and everyone else doing more work. This is not only a performance issue with that "slacker" employee but also a leadership issue, likely created by avoiding this potentially contentious situation in the first place and waiting for the "right time" to address it. Or maybe not being aware that the situation exists at all.

Another cause of team troubles is when work processes are defined, but they aren't followed. You want wiggle room for creativity and innovation, and you also need consistency in the results created by following the process. If the teams are not following the defined work methods, it could be a training gap or a lack of accountability. Generally, accountability is first established by the leader. Peer accountability develops between team members when the team dynamics are healthy, empowering, and productive. (More on those dynamics in Chapter 5.)

For example, one of my clients invested many hours into creating a comprehensive workflow. It identified each step of their process and the leader responsible for each step. On paper, it made sense. The missing piece was *how* to put it into practice because it meant the leadership team had to change how they did their own work and how they led their own teams. That required changing their thinking about how the process worked and their own role in the workflow.

This leadership team struggled with making changes to their daily routines so that they could adapt to a more productive workflow that respected the interdependencies between groups. Some were stuck in the mindset of "just getting it done" and "we don't have time to do it differently." It was frustrating for some of these leaders who were adapting and changing to see the others stay stuck in "that's the way we've always done it." Everyone must be willing to step up and be uncomfortable. If you, as a leader, struggle with change, how do you think that translates to your teams? (We'll talk more about motivating and navigating change in Chapter 8.)

Team troubles can also arise when there's a mix of "old" and "new" employees. Nope, I'm not referring to age. I'm talking about employees who have been with the business for a long time versus those who are new to the company. I've seen the friction this creates, especially when you layer a business merger on top.

It becomes the "old way" versus the "new way" and morphs into "they don't get it" thinking across the business. People shut down and stop talking, or the communication becomes extra polite and not at all productive. The grapevine rules the company, which is not an efficient or reliable source of information.

Whatever the desired business results of the impending changes, it's arduous to create them as people retreat into how they did things before and avoid anything new, including new colleagues. My background includes having navigated ten mergers in ten years, so I've dealt with this particular issue in my own professional path, as well as guided clients through it. The next chapter focuses on how to change business results when facing different types of challenges.

CHAPTER 3

THE CHALLENGE OF CHANGING RESULTS

*There's a direct connection between
how you lead and the results created.*

When I ask clients questions like:

- *What's happening in the business right now?*
- *What's good about that?*
- *What needs to be different?*
- *What is off track?*
- *What is absolutely working really well right now?*
- *What is missing that you wish was happening?*

. . . I usually receive a range of answers.

Of course, financial performance is always one of the first things mentioned. It's either too slow or not enough, or costs are too high. Sometimes, the answer is growth is happening at a pace that's hard to keep up with. Rapid growth is a great challenge to have, yet it's still a challenge.

What I find when I dig deeper with clients is the real topics of their concerns are related to how they function inside the company, meaning how they function as leaders and how their teams function. And what they see happening in the business that's puzzling. And how it feels to lead this organization. And how others feel when they work there.

All these thoughts lead to the questions: What results are being created? Are those the desired results?

Causes of Undesirable Results

If business priorities are always changing, it's hard to keep up. If it's hard for you, the executive, to keep up, imagine what happens with your leadership team and employees. They don't have access to the same business information that you do. Even if you share it with them, they don't *live in it* the same way you do.

Their viewpoint of the company is entirely different from yours. They are focused on implementing the last round of priorities they were given. When you change them, again, it can be difficult to pivot.

Related to changing priorities is changing deadlines. Or missed deadlines. We know that lining out the steps to complete a big project is essential to its completion. But when you change a key component in the middle of the project, it throws off the whole project, not just that component. If missing deadlines is a common occurrence for your company, there's more going on than just time management. This is one of the scenarios that inspired me to develop the *5 Pivotal Principles for Leading Deliberate Growth®* that are covered in the next chapters.

Next let's talk about the duplication of work between people. This one always leaves my leaders scratching their heads. *How did that even happen? And how didn't we know it was happening?* You might think this is only an issue with large organizations. The odds are higher for large organizations, but I've seen it happening in my clients' companies that have fifteen employees as well as my large company clients. A lack of leadership applies to any size organization.

A related issue is when that project goes totally awry, and you have to redo things. Rework is a very costly and preventable expense. Yep, I said *preventable*. The cause of rework is basically a problem with leadership and communication. Sorry, that might have stung a little.

Rework is one of the reasons I coach leaders and decided to write this book—because the solution to rework exists in leadership. I didn't say it is the sole responsibility of the leaders. Part of it lies in leadership—and that includes you, the executive leader(s), plus the leadership team, VPs, directors, managers, supervisors, team leaders, and whatever levels of leadership exist inside your organization. It is also within every employee in your business. *Every employee* contributes to causing rework or contributes to preventing rework.

If you are missing deadlines and changing project priorities, it probably impacts the customer or client in some way. Are your service levels at risk? Does this put any contracts in jeopardy? Yes, the client changing their mind about their product or system requirements might be contributing to the problems. Use your leadership skills to navigate that conflict without being confrontational to get back on track.

Productivity Issues

Battles Between Teams

In all industries, there's a common battle between sales and operations. I've experienced it in my corporate life and see it in my clients' organizations—what you sell versus what you produce and the differing viewpoints of what's possible. Operations wants to be mindful of costs, and they should be. Sales wants to sell things that the client/customer will buy, and that makes sense too. Innovative sales finds new client/customer problems that the company can solve. The rub happens when sales goes off the rails without a discussion with operations, or if operations clamps down on expense management, halts new service delivery methods, or interferes with production timelines at the expense of the customer relationship.

Both groups or each individual just assume the other will "never get it," so no one bothers to talk to each other. So, the productivity in both groups drops while they prepare for battle with each other. What does that accomplish toward the business goals or even the goal of the project? *Nada.* It's an energy-consuming and stress-inducing waste of time. This doesn't just happen between sales and operations. It's just a common example I see across all industries and business types. Stop this madness!

The viewpoints of each group are valid. Both create better innovation. Both are essential to the successful function of the company. Get in a room and decide to talk with each other without assumptions. (We'll talk more about getting out of your own way so you can communicate in Chapter 7.)

Why Don't They Understand Me?

I spoke to a frustrated group of CFOs and other financial professionals when asked to be the keynote speaker for an international finance executives association. One of their members saw me speak at an international professional women's association and referred me to this diverse group. Her mission was to expand their leadership aptitude beyond their technical knowledge of financial issues and opportunities.

A common question was, "How do I get other people to 'get it' when it comes to company finances and managing expenses?" The simplest answer is to put it into the language of the person you are talking with instead of crafting the conversation like you're talking with someone who thinks like you. It's a common blind spot in all types of relationships that we communicate like we are talking to ourselves. We aren't.

If people don't understand what you are saying, they find out through the grapevine because the direct communication avenues are inconsistent. You might think that's good because it shows people have built relationships. And that's true, except they are likely consulting with people who aren't directly involved with the project, which actually interrupts the project itself and consumes time in the company that could be used on higher priorities.

Training Gaps

If training isn't a priority, your people don't have enough or the right technical training to do their jobs. Leaders often assume their people know things that they don't. And, unless the environment is one where you are allowed to ask a question that might make you look uninformed—or worse, stupid—no one will admit they don't know things.

People who lack training spend more time doing their work because they have to figure everything out themselves. It's quite risky, actually, because you don't really know if their interpretation is accurate, and depending upon the complexity of your industry, it can be highly problematic. An alternative is that they involve more people in doing their work because they don't know how to do it themselves.

Unless this is intentional on-the-job training, it consumes the time of people who aren't responsible for training someone else. The person genuinely trying to understand their job probably feels like they have to apologize all over themselves for not knowing something they should have learned through training. Except they didn't receive training or enough training, or it wasn't timely.

Of course, one of the solutions is evaluating the environment to ensure people speak up when they need something. The other piece is to provide training and make it a priority for people to be able to participate in it.

Training gaps can also create conditions where people spend time wondering what everyone else is doing, or they wonder if everyone else is getting their work done because they are waiting on pieces they need to do their part. How do those things relate to each other? For some people, it seems like they have to pick up the slack a lot for the new person or even for the person who took on a more challenging project or role.

You'll want to look into whether you have a training gap or a communication issue. This symptom of poor productivity can happen whether you're all in the office or virtual. It can be more of a concern if you're virtual, given people aren't walking down the hall to ask a question. Creating some communication "rules" can help with that. Chapter 7 is devoted to communication. As I mentioned, don't skip ahead. You'll be far more effective faster as you continue reading the chapters in order.

Culture and Environment Challenges to Creating Desired Results

If it feels like pulling teeth to get answers to what you need, it's hard to get work done, and there's always some sort of battle before you make any decisions. Or it might be that you're getting things done, but it seems to take longer than needed. Or maybe you even set the expectations, have the meetings to review the goals, and get into the basic implementation steps a little, and still, there always seem to be *internal* roadblocks that leave you thinking, "Shouldn't this be easier?"

Chaos has become a "normal" way of life there. It just feels like everything has to be done right now, like, right now. If everything is a priority, nothing is a priority. If the whole page is bolded, then nothing is bolded because you made it all the same importance. Chaos is created by uncertainty. You don't know what they are doing, they don't know what you are doing, and the expectations from yesterday are not the same as today. So . . . your teams either just wait for you to make up your mind, putting deadlines at risk, or they spin with you, and then you all wonder why things don't get completed.

If the leaders are constantly living with high levels of stress and pressure, it is a constant distraction. This energy-draining distraction is like a rock in your shoe. You know it's there, but you don't bother to stop to get it out. Are you thinking that's ridiculous? Why would anyone walk around with a rock in their shoe? Good question. What if you chose to stop long enough to get the rock out of your shoe? Find the cause of your constant stress and what you can do about it. Your stress is felt by your team. Resolving it helps you, and it helps them.

One cause of the stress could be that you don't quite believe that your leadership team knows how to run the business, and changing that seems daunting. So, you continue to do more than you should and be involved in more projects than you need to because stopping to teach them things takes too much time. As the saying goes, if I had a nickel for every time a client told me they don't have time to teach people something . . . I could have retired years ago. I didn't say making time is easy peasy. I am saying it is absolutely worth it when you choose to do it.

In one client's case, the owner was convinced that there was no possible way that they could squeeze in training for his people. His leadership team was experienced, so they knew they "should," but didn't see a way for that to happen without putting work completion at risk. The thing is, if you want to grow the business, you must grow your people's knowledge and skills.

With a grumble, they said they would figure it out. And they did. It was time to get creative. The solution I coached them through was to *ask* the people who needed to participate in the training how to get their work done. The idea that surfaced was that they could be backups for each other while the other was in class.

This business owner in a professional service industry was shocked at that recommendation by his employees! He hadn't even considered this possibility because he was worried about the weight of putting two people's work onto one person, even for a few hours per week. He meant well because he was concerned about putting stress on his people. As it turned out, his people were waiting for him to get out of the way so they could get the education they needed. Everyone had the same intention—to do their work even better. However, this leader's mindset and assumptions were blocking that progress.

This example is evidence of an environment that is built to survive, but not necessarily built to thrive. Survival is only about what's happening today, or this hour, or in the next ten minutes. Thriving still completes things today, though the viewpoint is more strategic. Environments built to thrive have business goals that have been conveyed to all employees, and the business lives by those goals. It's not that things can't or don't change; it's that you have a foundation to work from. If you are in survival mode, it's only about who needs what right now and not planning or thinking about the rest of the year, month, or even this week.

I spent ten years in survival mode, more than I care to admit. For ten years, I was taking care of my own life plus two different parent households in different states. This is another time where I want you to learn from my experiences, whether you've taken care of aging parents or not. The problem here is that I slid in and out of survival mode. There were times of thriving, like when I earned some prestigious awards during that period. One was the *Excellence in Practice Award* for *Coaching and Mentoring* from the Association for Talent Development.

Yet, during that decade, it felt like my life wasn't my own because it wasn't. I've seen leaders feel like that during especially rapid growth or unexpected industry changes. You're focused on making sure the business survives those opportunities or obstacles. Changing your mindset may not change the type or amount of work that needs to be done, but it does change how your *energy is consumed*. That is the lesson I'm sharing now. Do this now. Understand this now. Dig deeper into your own mindset and take steps to help yourself be in thrive mode. Your team will feel it too. I will continue to share more about why that matters in later chapters.

You and your leadership team may feel like you lack some leadership abilities necessary to be as effective as you intend to be. To achieve this, you must understand the impact of leading by example, what delegating really means, adjusting your mindset, managing priorities, and cultivating teamwork. Take a breath. It's okay.

You might have even already invested a lot in leadership development for yourself, and you and your team are still having some of these issues in this book. First, celebrate that you've invested in developing your leadership skills. They are simply not being used effectively, and that's the next step—to learn to properly use the leadership abilities you've acquired, gain new ones, and expand your understanding of their impact.

You and the other leaders that I work with all have good intentions. You all want to develop yourselves and provide a safe and empowering environment for your employees. *The brutal truth is that you may lack some knowledge about yourself and how you lead.*

The Challenge of Changing Results

Before founding my executive coaching and leadership development company in 2010, I worked in small businesses, startups, and large corporations. I thought larger companies would have better leaders. They supposedly have more resources to invest in developing their leaders, so they would be doing that, right? Um, nope. In my experience, the lack of leadership aptitude was evident in startups and small and large organizations. The larger the company, the more complex the organizational structure, and the worse it got without leaders who knew how to lead. In some cases, there were leaders who knew how to lead, but they reported to leaders who didn't.

Want to know how to lose your most promising emerging leaders? Or the middle tier people you have your eye on for succession planning? The fastest way to lose them is to be the executive leader who doesn't know how to lead, meaning they can outperform you in leadership. You lack some mindset and leadership style knowledge and expertise that they need to feel empowered and engaged.

If this struck a nerve, I'm glad you're here to learn! And it's okay to go to your teams, admit you're learning new things, and engage with them in the process. They will respect you for the candid conversation and vulnerability. Be sure you convey the value they have as people and as leaders in the company and how important they are to the business. If they really are the future of the company, start the conversation sooner rather than later, or you might lose them while you wait.

In the context of this book, I'm only discussing your professional life, though I invite you to consider how my *5 Pivotal Principles for Leading Deliberate Growth*® could also help you in your personal life. Rarely has a client told me that they only use what they've learned in coaching programs with me exclusively in their work.

In the next chapter, we'll begin the exploration of the *5 Pivotal Principles for Leading Deliberate Growth*®. The first principle is the antidote to turning off autopilot, which I've named *Lead Not React*™. Are you ready to grow your leadership power? The next chapter is the first step.

CHAPTER 4

LEAD NOT REACT™
PIVOTAL PRINCIPLE FOR LEADING DELIBERATE GROWTH® #1

No one grows tucked securely inside their comfort zone.

THE SECRET TO TURNING OFF AUTOPILOT, RESOLVING TEAM TROUbles, and getting business results on track is this: The leader is the solution. The leader is also the problem.

The good news is if you are the problem and you are the solution, you can choose which one you want to be! You have absolute control over whether you are the solution or the problem.

You already know that you want to create an environment where you and your teams are seen, heard, and valued. That develops a culture where trusted teamwork is the normal mode of operation, and creating the desired results flows more easily.

Where to Begin

In my experience coaching executive leaders, reconnecting with your bigger reason for being a leader is the best place to begin. My intention is to reconnect you with why being a leader matters to you, and how that contributes to your own motivation.

Ask yourself: If you own the business, why this business? If you lead the business, why be a leader? What is it about this business and this role that stirs a deeper purpose for you? Another way to think about it is this: Why does it matter to you to become a better leader? What makes it important for you to focus on improving the business for your teams? What does growth represent to you? There are no expectations of what the answer "should" be. This isn't a test of some kind. Your answers are your answers, so be sure they are true for you.

Likely, you have personal reasons for yourself and your family. Perhaps it's the stability of lifestyle, flexibility, or that the industry is important to you or allows you to support causes that you are passionate about. Or something else entirely.

Let's take it a step further. What about your *team's why*? Have you ever asked your employees what makes them choose this company to work for? What they like the most about the role they have? What their vision for their career might be?

Whenever I'm working with a group of leaders, these are the questions we address in the very beginning. I find that it centers each person on the root reasons for working where they work and being committed to becoming better leaders. Their energy drops into their hearts instead of swirling around in their heads, and the discussions become much more real and authentic when they begin with, "What are we all doing here anyway?"

The answers to those questions form the motivation to *Lead Not React*™.

Understand Your Mindset

The next piece is understanding your own mindset. How you think about yourself, the problem, situation, person, obstacle, or opportunity is the starting point along the process of making it better (or making it worse). How you think about it automatically sets the course for the actions that will be taken. Understanding your mindset and the resulting choices and behaviors also explains why you do things the way you do.

If you believe that "no one else can do this," then you will forever be the one doing that. If you choose to shift that perspective into "this can be taught," now you have opened yourself up to the opportunity to delegate that work to someone else. If your viewpoint is that it can be taught, but "there's never time for training," you will remain trapped by what you believe are scheduling complications.

Calendar issues are real things. I'm not saying they aren't. I am saying that if you choose to be handcuffed by the belief that there's never enough time, then that will continue to be the primary source of stress for you. That might seem like a simplistic example, though I find that in mindset work, I need to slow way down in the discussion. Some of you have worked on mindset before, and some of you haven't. Nonetheless, remember to read this book without assumptions or judgments. Choose to set your perspective to being *curious* about how this could help you. I'll go deeper into this in this chapter, but don't skip ahead. It's important to have a thorough understanding of each piece that solves the puzzle.

Think of a leader you admire. What are the reasons you respect that leader? What are the characteristics of that person that contribute to your impression of them? Maybe it's their voice, how they speak, their demeanor, what they support that you also value, or how they handled a situation. Those are the things you can see. Those are the *visible* things that others can notice. I promise there are *invisible* things that make the leader effective. Those are the things that you don't see and can't observe.

If you have an opportunity to talk to them about their journey, you might be surprised to learn the steps they have taken to develop themselves: the continuing education classes for their profession, the mentors they have had in their career, the executive coaching they have embraced to build their self-confidence as the "boss" or "the one in charge" or "the one with the most responsibility," along with specific focus areas like how to think like a leader, be a better listener, and think strategically. Plus, transforming their leadership style by discovering their blind spots, understanding their impact on their teams, and finding what mobilizes the business results.

If this is a leader you admire, they likely have developed a Growth Mindset versus a Fixed Mindset. They likely have Empowering Beliefs versus Limiting Beliefs and Power Sources versus Power Blocks.

Unexpected events are the best test of your mindset and resilience. When something you didn't anticipate happens, good or bad, what viewpoint do you immediately have first? Are you the person who only sees all the problems and reasons something will never work? This means you are operating from a Fixed Mindset, Limiting Beliefs, and Power Blocks.

Or are you the person who can step back and strategically examine the whole scenario from a broader viewpoint? Lead with a Growth Mindset and identify problems while not being ruled by them? Use Empowering Beliefs to cultivate the possibilities and see the potential that could be created from whatever the situation may be?

When I first started coaching an experienced executive leader, she was entirely stuck in "how things were." She could not see herself or the new position she was in from any other perspective. Her language in describing the complexities at work was rooted in her own past and seeing the current opportunities through the bias of that lens. It tainted every decision she made as she attempted to unearth and reconnect with her own value. It was heartbreaking to me to hear how this brilliant leader had backed herself into a corner with so many limits on her own potential.

Fortunately, she engaged in working with me because she knew this was no way to live but couldn't get herself out of this mindset by herself. We worked together so that she could voice for herself all the impactful initiatives she had led in her career and the feedback she had received from her teams and colleagues. We dug up her willingness to speak up for herself, and she remembered why she loved to lead. Her career path began to unfold in ways she could not have imagined. This is one of the reasons I love what I do. This leader has impacted hundreds of lives and will continue to impact hundreds more. But first, she had to stop reacting and restart leading with an empowering mindset and belief about herself.

What You Make Things Mean

Along with how you look at things, another critical piece of Lead Not React™ is what you make things mean. It's crucial to examine the meaning you assign to a situation, event, person, obstacle, or opportunity. If something has been a pattern, do you automatically assume that's what is happening now, or do you consider the possibility that something might be different? If a person has behaved poorly in the past, do you label them and expect them to do it again? If something is working really well, do you leave room for it to go even better? Do you participate and then allow the situation to unfold, or do you automatically dredge up the past and look for evidence that it's repeating itself?

The *starting point* in your mind creates the train of thought that leads to decisions. Those decisions lead to the actions that are taken. Will those actions take you down a productive path or create rework?

Self-Leadership and Self-Confidence

Everything begins with the leader. This can be considered good news or bad news, depending on how you choose to look at it. See what I did there??

Self-leadership is a requirement to become more effective with others. In order to be a better leader of your teams, you first need to lead yourself. Yes, it begins with you. It's like the instructions we receive when we fly: "Put your own oxygen mask on first." If you want your teams to comprise more productive employees, you need to become one first.

The root of self-leadership is self-confidence, the belief in yourself that you can do something. Or the belief that if you mess something up, you are resourceful and can address whatever scenario just emerged. Genuine self-confidence is when what you believe about yourself is felt on the inside and portrayed on the outside—how you show up in the world matches how you feel in your body. It's important to clarify that you can still be rooted in genuine self-confidence despite being nervous about something.

When I was asked to speak for a college commencement ceremony, I didn't hesitate to accept the invitation. A staff member of the college saw me speak at another event and asked me if she could recommend me. Then they called! I knew I could engage an audience that size. When I got to the building and saw the sea of chairs in front of me, my stomach twisted in knots, and my breathing got really shallow. This was a case of nerves in the moment caused by being pushed out of my comfort zone and speaking in front of the largest audience I had ever had.

Thankfully, I had friendly faces with me who could help me recenter into my own power. I was there to deliver a message, and that's exactly what I was going to do. I was so honored when people sought me out after the ceremony to thank me for my meaningful twelve-minute talk. I cried with pride when I got to the car. I had touched people's lives that day. I did that. My twisted stomach wasn't a crisis of confidence. It was living the excitement of expanding my own speaking potential.

As a leader, consider scenarios or situations where you get a case of nerves. Is it around a certain person, situation, or topic? Is it a one-time thing or an ongoing issue? We're looking for the themes and whether this is a growth edge that's pulling you forward, like me speaking for the college commencement ceremony, or a pattern that's holding you back. In one client's case, it was a pattern with a particular person. Every time this leader in education had to present to a group when this particular person was participating, it made her mouth dry, and it was difficult for her to speak.

It turned out she was assigning meaning to him he didn't earn. Yes, he was a community authority, though he had no authority over her, even though she unconsciously assigned him that much power. See how easily that could happen, and you're not even aware of it? Until she started working with me, she was unaware this was a power block for her. She just knew that something "was off" with him, and it bugged her. It turned out it wasn't about him. It was about her perception and what she *assumed*.

The key is to build that inner confidence so that you continue to step outside your comfort zone and move forward into the leader you are becoming.

The Root of Self-Confidence

Self-awareness is critical to develop into a better leader. Genuine self-confidence comes from an inner knowing about your strengths, identifying and converting your blind spots, and building your emotional intelligence. The most important component is the *inner* belief in your value as a human and as a leader. When you have that within yourself, it can be seen and felt by others.

The most common mindset gap I've observed in executive leaders is a gap in their emotional intelligence, often referred to as EQ. Proper mindset and emotional intelligence are crucial for people to get along with each other, whether they engage in or value teamwork, and for navigating conflict within themselves and with their teammates. In fact, according to the World Economic Forum's "Future of Jobs Survey 2020," EQ is one of the top skills needed in business in 2025.[1]

Building your self-awareness about how you process your own emotions, and how others process their emotions, is the first solution to navigating your own work. It's also the first step to getting more comfortable delegating instead of doing it all yourself, and generating more collaboration in your teams. Are you going to be uncomfortable working on your emotional intelligence? Yep. No one grows tucked securely inside their comfort zone.

Emotional intelligence is something you can learn about. It's something that you can study if you choose. It boils down to understanding whether you Lead or React when things happen, good or bad. If you tend to react, fly off the handle, get loud, get quiet, disappear, get angry, withdraw, hide in your office, or become more stoic, it's likely driven by

---

[1] ÖZKAN, Metin. "The Future of Jobs Report 2020 - EPALE - European Commission." EPALE, May 6, 2021. https://epale.ec.europa.eu/en/resource-centre/content/future-jobs-report-2020.

a strong emotional response full of negative emotions. Reacting could also look like acting like everything is grand, amazing, and stupendous while you brush off the details and ignore the obvious problems right in front of you.

If you're worried, scared, frustrated, annoyed, stressed, bored, exasperated, or at your wit's end, you could be making fast decisions entirely based on speculation and without checking any facts. If you make decisions and take action from any of these reactionary mindsets, you are causing unnecessary stress for yourself and confusing your team. They don't know what to believe, and they don't want to deal with you until you return to some form of grounded leadership mindset. Even if it's not what they would say to your face, that's what they are thinking.

Think Like a Leader

When you are in the **lead** mode of Lead Not React™, you are squarely centered in a Growth Mindset and Empowering Beliefs and on your way to intentional actions that create *Deliberate Growth*®. You are not burying your head in the sand. You can see there are obstacles, but you don't start there.

A leader who is actually *leading* begins with a strategic viewpoint. This comes more easily to some than others. Wherever you are with this, that's okay. I've coached detail-oriented and analytical leaders on how to become better strategic thinkers, and I've coached strategic thinkers on how to become more mindful of details.

This is not about becoming a different person. It's about becoming a more empowered version of yourself as you develop a deeper awareness of yourself, how you think, and how you process emotions. It's about the domino effect on your teams when the leader becomes a more powerful version of themselves. Your teams notice, and it gives them permission to do the same.

When you shift out of reacting and into leading, and expand your emotional intelligence, you start to recognize the source of your viewpoint as you acknowledge how much or how little emotions influence your choices and how you communicate.

Thinking like a leader means accepting the responsibility that your decisions impact the business, all the employees, and you. If you are a new executive leader, you might still be wrestling with this fact. As an experienced executive leader, you might already "know" this, but it might still be challenging. It's okay. Just own your truth so that you have a clear picture of where you are starting from today.

Deeper thinking goes beyond the analysis of the situation into the emotions of the situation, aka developing your emotional intelligence about yourself and your team. Are you feeling confident, confused, bewildered, frustrated, empowered, excited, uneasy, informed, seen, valued, or dismissed? What is your team feeling? Will the choices you make create more ease or make things confusing for you and for your team?

Navigating the truth of your own emotions and those of your team is part of leading. Recognizing how emotions impact how we think, behave, decide, and take action is a fundamental factor in understanding humans. Yep, this can be complicated because humans have diverse gifts, strengths, blind spots, and challenges. Developing your self-awareness can help and is the best place to begin.

Self awareness as you think like a leader also includes understanding your own biases. We all have biases, and we use them without consciously thinking about it.

I'm a Kansas City Chiefs football fan. Does that mean I think the other NFL teams are bad? In my case, no. For other NFL fans, the answer could be yes. For me, what it means is that when I meet another Chiefs fan, we automatically have something in common. Same goes for you. Meeting someone who shares a common interest with you means you have something to talk about. Something to bond over. It might even help make that person memorable. Humans naturally seek others who understand them, so when we find people we share something with, we bond with them.

This common interest automatically forms a bias or a filter for information. Other factors that develop our self-created biases are based on our own life experiences—where we live, how we grew up, our education, our hobbies, what we value, our interests, our lifestyle, our worries, successes, challenges, concerns, support system, and the biases of the people in our lives, among other things. When we hear people share things, we are listening through our self-created filter or bias. Everyone does this. Everyone.

It is a *conscious* choice whether we judge something through our bias or become curious about it and explore it. Using our bias is a form of a Fixed Mindset that creates Limiting Beliefs that I mentioned earlier. Becoming curious is using Empowering Beliefs through a Growth Mindset, where possibilities are open and explored. Sometimes, we are judging others or the situation. Sometimes, what we are judging is ourselves. And the bias we are applying limits our own potential to grow as a leader and develop the performance of our teams. If the leader is limiting themselves, that belief permeates the team and limits them as well. No leader I coach wants to limit anyone's potential, including their own. This is why it's so critical to understand how easily and unconsciously it can happen.

An executive leader with thirty years of experience was working through a serious crisis of confidence. That's not how this client described it when she first came to me. She said things like, "I'm burned out with the hours and the politics getting thicker," "I feel like I have no voice," and "Others are making decisions for me." She said she needed to re-fall in love with the job because she was exhausted by the turmoil and didn't feel like she had any influence to change it.

Through our work together, this leader in a scientific industry expanded her span of influence and was invited to strategic meetings three levels above her. Given she was the CEO of her division, with about 325 people reporting up through her, you get the idea that this was a very large organization. The size of the business isn't the point.

Absorb the leadership issue as I continue so that you recognize any lessons that might resonate with you.

She was leading, but not by thinking like a leader. Her rush to lead was so strong that she forgot to do things she knew her team needed, like regular team meetings, recognition for a job well done, and support for navigating difficult client expectations. Her first instinct was always to analyze the data and the science. While she knew the people were important and valued the people, how she was leading didn't demonstrate that to her team.

On top of that, she had totally forgotten her own value. She was disconnected from all the achievements she had made on behalf of this company over the last three decades. Her expertise originated the techniques that were used and built the entire location she now led.

Our work together explored her emotional intelligence, grounded her into believing in her own value, guided her to leverage her specific strengths, and changed how she saw herself and her role. She assessed that the change in her inner confidence rose by 30 percent, and her stress went down. She said she could see the ripple effect happening when her team commented on the change in her energy, and her effectiveness in navigating difficult decisions. She noticed that her team became more decisive in the team meetings that were now being held regularly. She was living in her own value and leading from that mindset.

As she expanded her circle of influence and was included in conversations that set the strategic direction of the business, her voice was heard. She was asked for her viewpoint. In one case, because she was in the discussion and spoke up, she saved the company $800,000 in one decision.

Blind Spots Keeping You on Autopilot

Doing It All Yourself: The Lone Wolf Syndrome

In my prior example, this leader had stopped asking her team for help. She was living as a lone wolf and assuming that was just how it was going to be. And the leaders above her had stopped asking for help, which means they were also attempting to function as lone wolves. Each layer of the organization became more worried about making things work and less trusting that anyone else could help. So, they hid within their own roles, deciding it was better than "bothering anyone else."

When you're a leader with these tendencies, instead of finally delegating projects others could be doing and should be doing, you continue to press on as if you cannot possibly ask someone else to do that work. Usually, with the excuse that you don't have time to teach them how to do it or the assumption that they would see it as being "dumped on."

I call this mentality the Lone Wolf Syndrome.

No one grows tucked securely inside their comfort zone. That includes you. And it includes your team. In fact, remaining in the comfort zone stunts company growth. Break the cycle of doing too much yourself. Do it today. Time to create a new habit. Pick one thing someone else could be doing and learn how to have the conversation to move that work to their responsibilities.

Delegation is one of the top areas I coach and teach on—regardless of the level of the leader I'm working with and regardless of the years of experience in that leader. In fact, delegation at all levels makes you more efficient. A tech company client eliminated a full-time hire as one of the leaders became so much more adept at capacity management and delegation that adding another person wasn't needed. This saved the company $125,000.

The intentions are good. You don't want to be perceived as that person who is living the "crap rolls downhill" method. I applaud you for that. But work is supposed to roll "down" (or across) into the organization. And that's a good thing because it gives others the opportunity for development. Often, leaders have experienced being dumped on in their careers, which is why it's so difficult to delegate to someone else. You've only experienced the really negative way this has happened.

***The secret that I teach my clients is
Delegate Means Develop, Not Dump.***

When you flip your thinking and flip your mindset into exploring what that could mean for you and your team, delegation becomes a way of leading that empowers everyone. It's not possible for the leader to do all the work. If you could do it all yourself, you wouldn't have a team. It's one of the reasons that delegating is an essential leadership ability to develop.

First, consider the work that you should no longer be doing as the leader. Next, evaluate what team should be responsible for that work. That's the first layer. Now, determine which person could be doing that work. You will need to involve the manager/director/VP/whoever is the leader of that team. Consider how asking that team/person to take responsibility for XYZ project provides an opportunity for them to develop new ways of thinking, expand their business knowledge, and build skills and their careers. That is what it means to *Develop Not Dump*.

There will be times when you ask someone else to do the work because the responsibility needs to move to them instead of you, the leader. It may not be a snazzy opportunity for development; it may just be a change in who owns project X. Let that be okay. Part of being in charge is understanding the capacity of your teams and yourself, and which team or department is responsible for what areas of work.

If you learn to delegate well, and your teams start to wonder what work *you* are doing, it could be a sign that they are not feeling valued by you. In this scenario, they do feel "dumped on." It could also be a sign that you are not communicating enough about the vision, mission, or purpose of the company. You're also not sharing what you are working on for the future of the business. I realize there may be times when that is not possible. Just make sure they don't feel like they are working their rears off, and you aren't noticing and just giving them more to do for no reason. You have a reason. Share it with them often and always recognize their efforts.

Leading in a Rush Versus Taking Time to Lead

I've talked about the rush to lead as a leadership mistake. Again, your intentions are good. The execution of how you go about leading is the flaw. Usually, it's because you aren't aware of yourself—it's a blind spot.

Investing time to *lead* your teams exponentially pays off for them and for you. I'll go into more depth about leading teamwork in the next chapter. For now, let's keep revealing the blind spots.

Shiny Object Syndrome

In this blind spot, frenzied decisions rule because the next new idea is the great cure for your business problems. Turmoil reigns as you endlessly change your mind. You drive your team crazy since they never know what they should be working on today.

When you Think Like a Leader, you make Strategic Decisions instead of decisions by default. This intentional path accelerates the outcomes created from consistent effort.

Sticky Situations

Breaking up with being on autopilot can appear to be the hardest part of becoming a better leader. Consider this: You are in control of how you lead; it just might seem like you aren't, which means we are back to you being the solution and the problem simultaneously.

You already know some areas that are keeping you stuck and preventing you from the next big thing you want to move on. Or maybe it's a blind spot, and you're not sure what's stopping you. How do you change when "you've always done it this way?"

Changing your ways can be done, and it can happen quickly if you allow it to happen. Yes, change can take time to really become a new habit. That's okay. The first step is to take a first step, however small. Habits are changed by accumulating small changes.

What's one thing you could change today that would break your autopilot thinking? The next meeting you have? The next email you write? How will you go about making that next strategic decision? Consider how you would normally approach it and then what you might be missing with that approach. That's a start.

Below is an exercise to help you explore how you have been leading up until now.

Self-Awareness Exercise: *The Effective Versus Efficient Assessment*

The purpose of this exercise is to create some awareness around your thinking patterns. These patterns reveal your automatic biases and your "go-to" viewpoint, as well as how you solve problems, see opportunities, navigate obstacles, and make decisions. This exercise brings to light how these thinking patterns impact your interactions, pace of work, and assumptions you make about others.

Where do you land on this continuum?

EFFECTIVE ——————————— EFFICIENT

© Copyright 2025 Center for Deliberate Growth®

When you are faced with a new situation, problem, or opportunity, what do you think of first?

Do you think in terms of time first?

Do you think in terms of steps or output first?

There isn't a preference for which side of the continuum you "should" be on. I have no intention of trying to make you into someone else; I only intend to show you your starting point and how you can proceed from there.

Efficiency Thinkers:

If your answer was thinking in terms of time, your tendency is to think in terms of efficiency. People in this group tend to think in terms of how much time something will take as the first or primary focus, then they think about steps or process.

Effectiveness Thinkers:
If your answer was about the steps needed, the output required, or what might interfere, you are thinking in terms of effectiveness. People in this group tend to think about the process and problem first and time second.

"It Depends" People:
People in this group might go from one to the other and back again. And it might "depend" upon the context of the situation. Don't cop out and just pick this option as a catch-all though. There is no right or wrong or best position on the Effective versus Efficient continuum, only what is true for you. To help yourself the most, really think about your tendencies.

How Does This Awareness Help You Lead?
Let's imagine how this affects your interactions with others and the assumptions you are automatically making. If you are an efficiency thinker focused on how much time something takes, except you are communicating with an effectiveness thinker who is thinking in terms of steps, how might that impact the interaction?

You are trying to get it done fast with a focus on time—both in that conversation and the plan for the initiative. The effectiveness thinker you are talking with is trying to explain what this initiative will take and wishes you would stop trying to make it fast. When they speak about steps or output, you are thinking, "That will take too long" or "We can't possibly need all those steps."

Both of you are wondering why the other person doesn't get it or understand what you mean, which leaves you both wondering how this will ever work. The good news is your differences can help create a more thorough solution . . . once you listen to each other instead of waiting for the other person to stop talking.

What if two effective thinkers or two efficient thinkers are talking with each other? You think the other person is a genius! Why? Because you are both programmed to start the thinking from the same fundamental place. The downside is that two efficiency thinkers will likely miss critical steps because they assume they aren't needed to create a good output. The advantage is that the decisions will be made quickly. Two effectiveness thinkers may take too long to make a decision as they overanalyze the options, though the solution will be well thought out and focused on high-quality output.

As a leader with a team, you already know that part of your success comes from your ability to work through others because if you could run the company by yourself, you wouldn't have a team. The next chapter combines what you are learning about yourself with insights into how to transform teamwork and its impact on the business.

CHAPTER 5

TEAMWORK TRANSFORMED™
PIVOTAL PRINCIPLE FOR LEADING DELIBERATE GROWTH® #2

Teamwork is a verb.

Teamwork is not a noun that sits on a shelf to be admired from a distance. It's a verb that requires consistent, *daily* action to keep it active and current . . . from everyone on the team, including the leader. The solution to lead *Deliberate Growth®* begins with you. Then, it stems from how you lead your team.

If you are a leader without a team of direct reports, you likely have a matrix team or a cross-functional team that you lead, either indirectly or directly. You still lead yourself and must work with others to get your own work done. This chapter will show some ways to deepen your influence.

Fact Versus Fiction in Team Leadership

You Are Always Leading
Team Leadership doesn't take a break. There's not a time when you are a leader and when you aren't. There are times when you may need to lead differently, have different energy, or deal with difficult situations. Even when you are in your office by yourself, you are still leading. That email you just sent. The DM you answered. The call you did or didn't take. Each decision demonstrates how you are leading, the degree of care you show for your people, and what you prioritize. Let's break this down a bit more.

Caring Creates Growth Power

It's okay to be a human and care about the humans who work for you and with you. It's okay to show your heart and let your people see it. In fact, it gives them permission to show theirs and share more about themselves. You'll learn about what they value and what motivates them when they feel comfortable sharing themselves. And they will learn that about you as well. This is all part of understanding your emotional intelligence (often referred to as EQ) and how you work with others.

Some of you don't want your team to know you that well. I caution against that wall you are putting up. Of course, they don't need to know everything there is about your life, interests, family, challenges, or adventures. You can certainly have boundaries about what you choose to share, though let yourself share something. You cannot expect to learn about your people if you won't be a little vulnerable and share about yourself.

If you're thinking, "I don't want to know that much about my people," I completely understand; there are some who will overshare, and you'll learn things you never wanted to know. Not everyone will do that. You might just be assuming that. That's a blind spot based on an assumption and bias that is rooted in you being uncomfortable dealing with people and their emotions. You'll say it's because you have work to do. And that's true. But it's primarily because you don't want to deal with their emotions.

You may recall that emotional intelligence is one of the most common mindset gaps I see in executive leaders. This is an example of that. Take a moment and consider that for yourself. Then continue. There's more to learn here, and as I say to my clients, I have your back.

Yes, there is a method to opening up about your life, especially if you haven't done it much. I'm actually an example of that. During the decade of taking care of two different households aside from my own, I didn't share much about my personal life. Taking care of parents with health issues and the complex logistics I was managing weren't exactly uplifting topics. I also figured that when I was working with clients and speaking at conferences, people didn't really want to know about my life. I was there solely to help them, and that was my focus.

I was wrong. They do want to know because they want to know about me. No, not everything about me because they were there to help themselves, but just enough to feel like they knew me a little beyond just the work I was doing with them. It turned out that including stories about my life in my talks helped my audiences relate to me more, not less. Did different people react differently? Of course. And your teams will, too. And that's okay. You can handle whatever happens. If you discover a gap in your mindset or your skills, this is where an executive coach can help.

So, what if you already do share things about your life? And you think it takes up too much time for people to just be chatting about things? Ask yourself: Does it really take up too much time? Or are you so focused on completion and functioning from a frenzied mindset that it just *appears* to take up too much time? I agree that an hour talking about the Super Bowl, World Series or your college basketball team is probably too much. Except . . . when it turns out that your business team has a lot of sports fans.

This can actually be a team-building discussion because your people are getting to know each other better. And if they are sports fans, they might understand the teamwork required for teams to function well. If not, it's an opportunity to draw some analogies to illustrate leadership and teamwork—and invite other topics or interests into the discussion. Investing time to "chat" doesn't change the project deadlines or quality expectations. It does change how the people who are doing the work for those deadlines and quality expectations function by expanding their understanding of one another and deepening trust.

Compete or Collaborate

One indication of a toxic company culture is if you avoid sharing about yourself because you're afraid it will be used against you. Um . . . if you're the executive leader, and that's your fear, imagine how your teams must feel. That is a clear sign of problems in the interactive dynamics inside your organization. If people are not driven by collaboration and pitching in to help each other, then they may be driven by competing with each other or working in silos. Which means they don't share information or decisions, and instead focus on who gets the credit, good or bad.

If this sounds familiar, your business is functioning in a Fixed Mindset with Limiting Beliefs that no one can be trusted, and it's "every person for themselves." Ick. I worked in this environment. It's awful. It's toxic because you spend so much energy trying not to get into trouble for doing your job that it makes it hard to actually do your job. People who perpetuate this kind of culture are not high performers, although they will convince you that they are. They work the people, not the goals, and they know "where all the bodies are buried," as the saying goes. That's the only power they have—not the power to do their own job well, let alone lead anyone else.

When the company culture is collaborative, people don't fear sharing. What are they sharing? Ideas, decisions, information, suggestions, and even a bit about themselves. They are willing to listen to others' ideas, be questioned and ask questions, and explore obstacles and ideas from a Growth Mindset based on Empowering Beliefs about themselves, their team, and the business.

In order to get to a more functional state of team collaboration, the leader of an organization must be honest about the situation as it stands right now. Some people may already perform in a collaborative way, while others may function in silos or be pricky competitors. Leaders must dig deep into their courage to make changes that might be difficult. It could be that some employees would benefit from an investment in professional development like coaching or training while others may need a performance plan. It might even be that some employees will do better if they are invited to work elsewhere.

One clue about whether your team competes or collaborates is to notice what they do when things go wrong. Do they go to each other **first**?

Do they work it through within the team first? This is an indication of trust within the team. Working within the team first means the team is a unit. Going elsewhere first likely means more rework as people make decisions and complete tasks without first being on the same page within their team.

You, the leader, need to own the part of this culture that you are creating. The first step is understanding more about how you lead and the impact your style has on you and your teams. Reflect on what you learned about your mindset and default leadership viewpoint in the *Effective Versus Efficient Self-Awareness Exercise* in the last chapter. Then, be willing to make changes to how you lead to address the blind spots you may have.

Pleasing Versus Leading

Some people feel a lot of internal emotional tension to please others. This internal friction creates the conditions where the leader is being directed by others. That isn't the same as leading others. The intentions of the "pleaser leaders" are good. What you think you are doing is helping people and making them happier at work. But pleasing people isn't leading them. It's doing whatever they say without much discernment about what they are asking or requesting and maybe even demanding.

If this sounds like you, shifting this tendency or habit requires you to dig deep. Get real with yourself. Are you actually discerning the situation to make a sound business decision? Or are you listening and agreeing to whatever this person wants because you are avoiding the potential confrontation—and not being liked—if you say no?

Get ready to be uncomfortable. It *is* possible to do things differently—to think differently, to behave differently, and to thrive through it all! You may recall the discussion on genuine confidence in the prior chapter. Take steps to build that within yourself and to trust that *you can* handle conflict and people not liking you all the time.

Those of you who don't have the "pleaser" tendency might know someone else who has it. Or you may even work with someone who has it.

After reading this section, reflect upon how you interact with them. Do you take advantage of their "pleaser" tendencies? Does that actually help you, your team, or your colleagues? Or does it lead to miscommunication later? A yes from a "pleaser" leader doesn't necessarily mean "yes." It might mean maybe, or it could mean a conditional yes, but they didn't share the conditions. And they probably didn't involve the other people who could contribute to solving the problem or exploring the opportunity.

If you are a "pleaser," lead yourself out of being a pleaser. And if you work with pleasers, gently coach them to slow down on saying yes to make other people happy and to share their real opinions. Their greatest value is in the truth you are missing out on because their inner confidence is so low. Invest in coaching to raise their confidence level so that they will convey their ideas to the team and to you.

A Willingness to Be Uncomfortable

As the executive leader, your inclination to stretch, expand, and grow yourself directly affects the degree to which your team is willing to do these things. This is why you need the leadership skill of Leading by Example. **Show** your team your growth edges, meaning the areas you are developing, so that they have permission to do the same.

A client in manufacturing struggled with a volatile employee. He avoided this direct report since it triggered a deep frustration within him that people would behave like that at work, or at all. This leader owned the fact that he responded the same way and hung his head about the heated exchange he had with this person in front of others. The truth was he didn't know what to do differently from what he had done already. He just knew that reacting in the same way his employees were behaving wasn't working. And he could see his team wondering why he wasn't doing anything about this obvious problem.

During our coaching work together, he explored his mindset. This leader was fixated on the assumption that this was a "problem employee." He hadn't considered that this was an issue with how he was leading, and that the solution actually began with him. It was "enlightening," as he put it, to learn that he had more influence on the situation than he realized.

What happened? The next time his employee blew up, this leader and I had already worked on his mindset and his emotional intelligence about himself, and he was able to change the situation. He knew that in that moment, he would not be heard.

So, he kindly exited the situation and allowed things to calm down. Then he went back later to have a conversation with this long-time employee about what he was trying to say, and how his message wasn't being heard because of his demeanor. People tend to stop listening when you start yelling. Instead, they get defensive and, especially in a work situation, embarrassed or ashamed.

Because this leader changed how he led the situation, this employee has not blown up since. He's worked with this individual on his own mindset and how he communicates, and discovered that he has had interesting ideas to contribute. His teammates have noticed the change, and it's reduced the stress for everyone—enough that they comment to the leader about it with heartfelt thanks for taking care of it. I'll talk more about listening and communication in Chapter 7.

Leading by All Head or All Heart

If you lead with all heart, all emotions, and all support, the business performance suffers as you are overly accommodating people's personal needs. If you lead with all head and logic, your people will not feel like they matter as humans, let alone employees. If they come to you about complex family issues or personal scenarios getting in the way of work, and you don't seem to care about that or care about them, they'll notice your lack of empathy. If the lack of caring continues, it reduces employee satisfaction and puts employee retention at risk.

Effective decisions are created by combining your head and your heart. You want to approach interactions with others with strategy and logic, plus care and concern.

It's alright to expect results from your teams *and* care about them as people. There's still work to be done, regardless of what's happening in people's lives. The question is how to balance valuing your employees as humans with the need for them to complete their work.

When people have life stuff happening, you know that might not make them as productive. It's your call how flexible you want to be with them. Make sure you are recognizing the impact of their change in productivity on their team and colleagues.

The "head" piece of the decision is about getting work done. The "heart" piece of the decision is about considering they are human. The more you combine both perspectives, the more you are developing your sense of emotional intelligence while maintaining accountability for business needs.

Team or Work Group

A group of people assigned to the same leader is a work group. They likely work together and cooperate because they probably need one another to do their jobs. This doesn't mean they function as a team. When problems happen in a work group, its members might be put into the same room to resolve them despite the mindset of the people being focused on themselves, and not on each other or the group as a whole.

A team is a group of people who consciously consider each other as each individual does their job. Each makes an effort to understand how their job impacts their teammates' ability to do their jobs. When problems arise, the team pulls together to solve them. When opportunities arise, they work together to explore the avenues to maximize them. Conflict and mistakes still happen in a group that functions like a team, though the resolution is less stressful since people focus on the issue at hand and don't take things personally.

High-performance teams do all of these things I just mentioned, and they do them more quickly. Rapid resolutions to problems happen because the level of *trust* is so high. The challenge in high-performance teams is if someone leaves the team, and the team needs to reset with a new member.

Healthy Team Dynamics

What do healthy team dynamics look like?

- The first and primary ingredient is trust because trust creates the safety to succeed, to fail, and to talk about all of it. Trust is so important that I created a T.R.U.S.T. Builds Teamwork Model, which will be explored in greater depth in just a minute.

- The team listens for meaning without assumptions and judgment.

- Speaking up with ideas is expected, and there's follow-through.

- Peer accountability develops as questioning oneself and questioning others is normal and not taken as a judgment of character, intellect, experience, or ability. It's given with curiosity and received as exploration.

- Preventing problems is a quality focus and happens more easily with a fundamental level of self-belief from each individual and within the group.

One of the reasons I'm a sports fan is seeing teamwork in action! During training camp, NFL Head Coach Andy Reid of the Kansas City Chiefs frequently mentioned aspects of leadership and teamwork. Coach Reid openly stated that he's not always right and wants people who speak up with well-thought-out ideas. He wants players who are good communicators and ask questions to learn things. He distinguishes between planning to win a game and coaching the players to maximize their potential to raise the performance level of the team. Both are critical elements for success. It's the same in business.[2]

Part of the regular process of an NFL season is having more players recruited than will make the team. This means coaches are always *observing* the players individually and as a group to watch for signs of teamwork, and to see if there's good communication by spotting exchanges between players. Coaches also observe those exchanges to see if it improves their attitude and performance or not. Are they the type who sulks if they receive negative feedback, or do they take it in stride and use it to get better? Does positive feedback puff up their insecure ego, or do they proudly use it as confirmation of a job well done and aspire to do it even better? Even if you aren't a sports fan, take the leadership and teamwork lessons from this analogy.[3]

I wouldn't suggest putting your team in pads and cleats on the football field to test this for yourself. However, you can observe your team in team meetings and then make some notes about who needs to grow a bit in their confidence or collaboration aptitude. You might even find a teammate who could coach them.

You may be thinking that you already observe your people. Good! What are you observing about them? Their strengths? Their complications in their communication? Something that bugs you? And what do you do with the observations? Are they part of growth and development conversations? Do you create avenues to share their strengths and areas of growth with them, or do you just keep all that to yourself and "work around it?" Whatever you do, development begins with building trust.

---

2   "Andy Reid Opening Training Camp Press Conference." Kansas City Chiefs, July 2024. *www.chiefs.com/video/andy-reid-opening-training-camp-press-conference-19045370.*

3   "Andy Reid: 'Not Everyone's Going to Make the Team, But Make It Tough on Us': Press Conference 8/5." Kansas City Chiefs, August 5, 2024. *www.chiefs.com/video/andy-reid-not-everyone-s-going-to-make-the-team-but-make-it-tough-on-us-press-conference-8-5.*

T.R.U.S.T. Builds Teamwork

Back to my model for building trust that I mentioned earlier. These five elements are the foundation for trusting yourself and trusting others. They create the healthy dynamics and psychological safety you want your team to have and *sustain*.

This might appear simplified, and that's intentional. When you can easily remember the five elements of trust, you are more likely to shift your thinking and actions to become aligned with them. Each element has its own power to create trust. When they are combined, *trust becomes durable*.

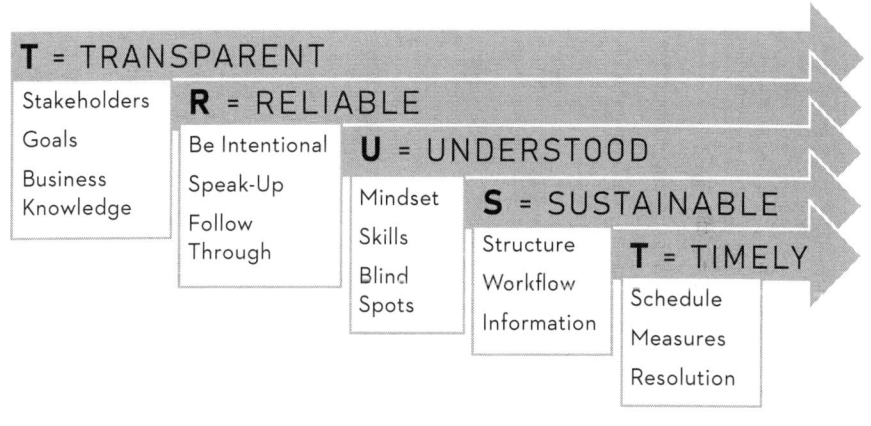

T = TRANSPARENT
- Stakeholders
- Goals
- Business Knowledge

R = RELIABLE
- Be Intentional
- Speak-Up
- Follow Through

U = UNDERSTOOD
- Mindset
- Skills
- Blind Spots

S = SUSTAINABLE
- Structure
- Workflow
- Information

T = TIMELY
- Schedule
- Measures
- Resolution

TEAMWORK IS A VERB

© Copyright 2025 Center for Deliberate Growth®

T.R.U.S.T. Builds Teamwork

TRANSPARENT	Share the real situation and your real thoughts and feelings, even when it's uncomfortable for you or uncomfortable for them. Also share what's happening in the business and the industry. People engage when they understand what's happening.
RELIABLE	Do what you say. It boils down to that. Prevent the unkept promises saga that I mentioned in Chapter 1.
UNDERSTOOD	Develop awareness of your own mindset around how you lead and how you communicate. Convey messages in ways *others* understand, not in ways that you would understand. Ask questions from a place of curiosity and listen for meaning without preemptive judgment.
SUSTAINABLE	Use the structures like Automatic Avenues of Accountability (explained later in this chapter) to your advantage. Share information others need to make decisions.
TIMELY	Be responsive. You want people to get back to you, so do the same. Measure what you want to grow. Promptly resolve open issues.

Building trust is not about how to get people to agree with you. Trust is about how you interact, speak to each other, listen, and consider the other's experience and perspective. Even between people who disagree, if they function with these elements, there is trust that they know where the other stands. And there's now respect for the other viewpoint because they know it's a real opinion shared by someone they trust, whether they agree with them or not.

Staying on the Same Page

It's not enough to get on the same page. The trick is to *stay there* from a strategic viewpoint that accounts for the purpose of the team, and the nitty gritty decisions and actions that are taken each day.

One strategic tool that can help is developing a *written* Team Charter (think strategic plan for your team) that includes Shared Commitments, Ground Rules, or Shared Agreements in how you want to function as a team. It includes the mission of the team and how it connects to the mission of the business, the goals of the team, and the dynamics of how you want to interact with each other. It could be a page, maybe two. You could have people sign the interactive dynamics part if desired. When there are changes in the team members, the Team Charter serves as a starting point for quickly bringing the new person up to speed. It also provides a starting point for revisions when a new person is added to the team or when someone is replaced after leaving.

In a project-based business, project management plans are designed to keep people on the same page when they are developed and actually followed. Some of the project managers are groaning right now because they know the effort it takes to write a complex project plan and then the frustration that ensues when it's ignored. Or when it changes frequently because the priorities weren't considered thoroughly enough in the beginning. Nevertheless, the project plan provides a guide. Of course, the plan is worthless unless it's communicated, discussed, and updated on a regular basis with all the relevant people.

Maximizing what I've named the *Automatic Avenues of Accountability* creates the structure you need to more easily stay on the same page. I'll talk more about how to use these in Chapter 7 when I go into more depth on communication. These alignment tools include *consistent* team meetings, project status meetings, employee communications, strategic retreats, department discussions, problem-solving or issue explorations, and growth and opportunity navigations.

Conflict: Your Team's Opinion of Their Leader and Its Impact on Productivity

We all know there's going to be conflict. It's "normal" when there's more than one human in a room. It's expected even. No two people are the same, thank goodness! What a boring world we would live in.

One of the classic conflict situations is having a difference of opinion with others when it comes to how to solve something. **First**, verify that you are solving the same problem. Often, when I'm working with teams who are struggling to discuss a situation, they aren't even talking about the same thing. Ever had a conversation, even at home, when you suddenly say, "What are you talking about?" and they say, "What are you talking about?" As I'm writing this book, I'm updating my house, and this just happened in my life last week. The contractor and I were not talking about the same thing at all. I was talking about a wall in the master bathroom, and he was talking about a wall in the guest bedroom. No wonder we had no idea what the other one meant!

The same thing happens in your team. If your team is wrestling to get on the same page, stop the conversation and verify that you are even solving the same thing—that how you see the problem or even what the obstacle is is the same thing. Start there. That alone will help you clarify where everyone stands. When you have healthy team dynamics, this discovery of not being on the same page could result in chuckles while you laugh at yourselves, get back on the same page, and go from there. Dynamics that are more siloed, like work groups, could result in hurt feelings, taking things personally, or the worry that one will be judged as stupid or uninformed. Know your group. Are you a team or just a work group? What do you want your group to be?

According to the Thomas-Kilmann Conflict Model, solving conflict is about two dimensions: the degree to which you are willing to cooperate and the degree to which you are willing to be assertive. Why am I using a conflict model from the 1970s? Because it's still relevant in human behavior. And it's one of the easiest to relate to. When I updated the curriculum of the organizational communication and leadership certification program for an international association, this is still the model that I included. [4]

When I discuss this conflict model with clients, I often exchange "cooperate" with "degree to which you're willing to be uncomfortable" because it creates the emotional dimensions needed. As a result, the two dimensions of conflict become the degree to which you will speak up and be assertive versus the degree to which you will stretch yourself emotionally to deal with what's happening in front of you.

The "pleaser" leader I mentioned earlier has a very low tolerance for being uncomfortable and a very low tolerance for being assertive. The team calls this leader the "yes" leader because they won't say what they really think or want and just agree to everything. These false promises come back to bite you—and your team—big time, not to mention the hours of wasted time deciphering what you really meant since you didn't actually share that part.

The leader who is highly assertive but has a low tolerance for being uncomfortable is usually loud, trying to cover the fact that they are uncomfortable. The team calls this leader arrogant, not knowing that this leader is fundamentally insecure and not fundamentally full of themselves. Arrogance arises from someone who is incredibly insecure, not someone who is incredibly confident. The team wastes time trying to work around the leader because they don't want to deal with them.

The leader who has a high tolerance for being uncomfortable but a low tolerance for being assertive is very frustrated and often feels defeated. They want to shake things up, but they are afraid to speak up. It might vary a bit depending upon who is in the room or the number of people in the room, but for the most part, they hold back their brilliance out of fear of failure. The team of this leader doesn't feel supported or understood since this leader won't go to bat for them or get

---

4   Jones, John E. "Thomas-Kilmann Conflict Mode Instrument." *Group & Organization Studies* 1, no. 2 (June 1976): 249–51. *https://doi.org/10.1177/105960117600100214*.

into a conversation that might feel confrontational because the leader doesn't trust themselves enough to handle the questions that might come their way.

The leader who has a high tolerance for being uncomfortable and a high tolerance for being assertive speaks their mind. The team loves it because they know where they stand and what's expected of them. This leader isn't afraid of collaboration, being questioned, or even being totally wrong. They love having a team of people who think of things they don't and challenge the status quo.

Consider for a moment . . . which category do you fall into? Consider your team. How do they generally function as individuals? What about as a group? How is that helping or hurting your communication? Your productivity? Your stress levels and that of the team?

A second-generation small business client who owned the company for several decades wanted to change the culture of the business. He represented a different generation of leaders and wanted the business to function according to his vision. One of the issues was that he was a "pleaser leader" through and through and knew this about himself. He actively avoided conflict and was known as the "yes man" by his team. He would rarely ask the questions he really wanted to know the answer to, and if he did, it was only after he worried about it for a few days first.

This pattern of stress and behavior was duplicated by his leadership team. They didn't tend to speak their minds—not at the time when problems could be prevented. Everyone was conditioned to be the hero during a time of client crisis, but no one invested energy into what could prevent the crisis in the first place. Each person did their job, but not with conscious awareness of how their productivity impacted the next person in the workflow.

When the owner communicated that they would implement seven strategic improvements to the business, this leadership team struggled to understand what he was suggesting. Their tendencies to keep their ideas to themselves and not ask questions of each other kept everyone in the dark. As I mentioned, sometimes the first step is to define the problem you're all trying to solve.

As we worked together, this team began to understand their interdependencies, trust evolved, and the stress levels in the team went down. In fact, this former pleaser leader shed three hours per week of worry and has "more confidence than he has ever had." The team spent less time glaring at each other in silence and more time asking questions and gathering necessary information. The risk of reworking the production schedule was incrementally reduced as they continued to explore the experience of working *with* each other instead of working in spite of each other.

Working through conflict is fundamentally about trust. See my T.R.U.S.T. Builds Teamwork Model above for a reminder. First, do all the people involved believe that there is a solution to be found? That doesn't necessarily mean that everyone will 100 percent agree with each other. Second, it's more about whether there is enough trust to have an honest conversation and discover a solution. Even if people believe there is a solution, without the trust to work on it together, people won't speak up with their ideas or comment on other people's ideas. When there is trust, people are free to question each other, disagree, and even laugh together on the way to determining a solution.

Team Leadership Blind Spot: Bottleneck Denial

This blind spot is rooted in the assumption that the lack of progress is caused by others while being totally unaware of your own impact. It means you sit at your desk and grumble about how other people are holding up your work without a clue that your choices are holding up their work. You are actually contributing to the bottleneck, and you don't even know it because you're so focused on what other people are doing. This Fixed Mindset is putting blinders on your thinking.

Your teams wait for the other shoe to drop because it always does in this blind spot. Why? No one is taking responsibility for the bottlenecks in productivity, so everyone is waiting for someone else to do something about it. The good employees, the team members you want to retain, will give up and leave because they are tired of waiting for the leaders to get it. The other employees work just hard enough to stay out of trouble.

When there's a light shined on this blind spot, the result is Clarified Purpose. Productivity soars as you take ownership of your role in creating the bottleneck and then remove it. You'll hear your teams sigh in relief. They will know what's going on now, and they will stop waiting on you. As you explore how this bottleneck was created, you'll learn about your strengths and growth areas as a leader and re-engage with your teams.

Sticky Situations

A common question posed to me is how to navigate asking for help versus interrupting your colleagues and consuming their time. First, what you ask about and whether you've tried to figure out the answer on your own matters. If not, that's just using their time instead of your own. It's most effective if you've already discussed these issues as a team, meaning it's part of the Shared Agreements you've developed.

Resistance in your team may be a sign that your leadership is challenging the status quo. That might be exactly what your business needs! And what your team needs. How do you address the resistance? This is actually about the team's resilience and tolerance for change. (We'll talk more about change in Chapter 8.)

In the following chapter, we'll address one of the most overlooked aspects of building growth: alignment. Whether there's alignment in your priorities and what your people work on makes or breaks your results. It seems so obvious, but I see gaps with every client.

CHAPTER 6

RECALIBRATE FOR RESULTS™: ALIGN PEOPLE, PRIORITIES, AND PROFIT
PIVOTAL PRINCIPLE FOR LEADING DELIBERATE GROWTH® #3

Actual alignment requires intentional thought and is often a blind spot.

GET MORE DONE FASTER. IT'S A COMMON GOAL OF AMBITIOUS leaders who are leading for growth in their business. Raise productivity to generate more results and grow the company.

As the saying goes, this is where the rubber meets the road. This is the chapter about the business results that are or aren't happening in the business. These are the issues that you can *see* happening—the results that you seek or the results that you are creating. My guess is since you are reading this book, the results are not necessarily working the way you want, or you're about to uplevel expectations a lot, and you're not sure how to lead to do this.

Alignment is where what you are trying to accomplish lines up with the effort and actions you are taking in the business, the measures of success (how you know what you are doing is working), and the resulting outcomes. Having alignment prevents things like saying you want to raise revenue and then spending your effort on managing expenses. Not wrong. Just not aligned. It seems obvious that these things need to line up, but this is a real example.

After listening to an experienced business owner discuss their goal of raising seasonal revenue to even out cash flow throughout the year, in the next breath and for the next twenty minutes, I watched this client map out an action plan to manage expenses. Is it wrong to manage expenses? Of course not, but the actions you take to manage expenses are not the actions you take to raise revenue. Managing expenses might expand profit, but it won't raise revenue.

Finally, in interrupting them, I reconfirmed their priority was raising revenue, which led to them looking at me with a quizzical look, like, "Yes, I just said that." *Yes, you did, and yet the last twenty minutes have been spent on action steps to manage expenses without any discussion about action steps to raise revenue.* Blank stares on all of the leaders' faces. Massive blind spot!

And here's the rest of the blind spot. While raising revenue was their primary focus—they didn't really know how to do it. They were very familiar with managing expenses and had years of practice doing that. Steps to raise revenue, like focusing on new sales, were far less familiar. The result? The leaders were unknowingly leading their teams down a path to manage expenses while they were telling them to raise revenue. No one knew what to do differently to raise revenue, and no one was saying that out loud.

This example illustrates the multiple layers of alignment.

First – Alignment with yourself – As a leader, as a team member, as someone committed to contributing to results. As someone who *knows themselves* and is willing to learn even more to understand the responsibilities that come with completing the work.

Second – Alignment within your team – The way your team functions or doesn't function. How your team needs to develop as a group and individually. As I discussed in the last chapter, teamwork is a verb and builds on T.R.U.S.T.

Third – Alignment with how the business functions – This level is how handoffs work between teams. It is also maintaining mutual understandings of the goals, priorities, and mission of the business, along with the results desired, and the results created.

In this client's case, they were misaligned in the leader's priorities, the direction they were taking the team, and the actions they were taking. The result? Expenses would have been managed, but frustration would have ensued because revenue would have been flat. They would have gotten to the end of the focused six months completely confused because the goal was to raise revenue, and it didn't happen.

Except . . . they were working with me, and I was helping them see the blind spots in how they were functioning as leaders, as teams, and as an organization.

Through my work with them, their seasonal cash flow went up by 20 percent because what they said their priorities were now aligned with the actions they were taking. I helped them map out a plan to grow their sales and showed them how to work with their teams to implement it.

Maybe your biggest business issues right now are frustration with constant rework or even the shocking discovery of the duplication of work. Alignment is the solution to these *preventable* problems. Some of you might be thinking, "YES, that is my issue right now!" Others are thinking, "I don't think we have much rework or duplication of work, so what does alignment have to do with my situation?" Everything.

Misalignment is the most expensive gap in business. What does that mean? Millions of dollars gush out of companies because of wasted effort, rework, duplication of work, high levels of stress due to misunderstandings, and energy being spent on the wrong things. And it's a *giant* blind spot for leaders because when you hear about it, you won't believe that it happens in *your* business.

If you are sitting there wondering about your own company because you aren't really sure of how your business functions, invest in making alignment deliberate as opposed to believing it to be something that "just happens." Why? Because if it's something that "just happens," it's something that when it stops happening, no one will know why. Because you didn't know you were doing it in the first place.

Alignment is the reason you don't have rework or duplication of work. Make it intentional. As I've mentioned, this book is about *Deliberate Growth*® using the *Pivotal Growth Principles* that I created. It's about being intentional, strategic, and engaging. This book is not about an "if it ain't broke, don't fix it" methodology. This view is totally unconscious, completely risky, and likely will blow up in your face at some point. It will be one of those situations where you think, "Why did that quit working? What was it we were doing? Was it one person doing it all, and that person left? And I had no idea how much they were leading the process for me?" If this is the case for you, it was a one-person solution and not a way of life you adopted to function better as a business. The fact that alignment requires intentional thought is often a blind spot.

Where to Begin

First step: Take a step back, not forward. Yep, step back. If you're standing right now, you could even physically move your body backward a step while you're reading. Or slide your chair back a bit.

The beginning of alignment actually starts with taking stock of where you are now—where you *actually* are now, not where you *think* you are or *assume* you are. That means you as the leader. That means your teams. That means the results that are or aren't happening in the company.

Alignment is not just goal-setting. Goal-setting is what you want to achieve in the future. It's definitely a key element, though by itself, it is not alignment.

Alignment allows you to achieve your goals, not the other way around.

The only way that alignment of people and priorities creates profits is when you step back and look at the whole picture: the good, the incredible, the amazing, the bad, the ugly, and the "what the hell was that?" Don't spend months on this. That will likely spiral you down rabbit holes that aren't valuable and just full of distractions. There's a fine line between dissecting and discerning information to make a sound decision. You don't want to overanalyze the options and procrastinate a choice because you are worried you'll be wrong, or wait for more information that isn't actually going to change anything. I'll show you which areas to focus on, so stick with me.

Preventing problems is a quality-based strategy versus dealing with whatever happens after the fact. Stepping back requires looking at the whole picture from a strategic perspective versus the tactical, in-the-weeds perspective. As the executive leader, you are automatically expected to handle the "big picture" of the business.

Looking at the "big picture" is often called *strategic thinking*. In fact, using my *Pivotal Principles for Leading Deliberate Growth*® helps you develop strategic thinking. Some leaders have more natural gifts in this area, and some don't. Regardless, strategic thinking is likely an area of development for you. Even those with natural tendencies benefit from some tweaks. At the executive and upper management levels, a tweak can shift the business. It doesn't need to be an overhaul of your abilities as a leader.

This does take intentional effort from a Growth Mindset. Set aside any Limiting Beliefs you have about strategy, planning, meetings, discussion, or exploration because you'll need all of those elements to create true alignment. We're not after perfection—we are aiming for excellence. Excellence is about doing things well. Be thorough, but don't get into analysis paralysis.

Perfection is about pleasing other people and not in ways that are productive. It's also about insecurity within yourself because you think the only way you are valuable is if it's perfect. I'm talking to my fellow overachievers. You don't have to be perfect to be valuable. You are valuable as you are right now. *You become more valuable with greater self-awareness and a willingness to step out of your comfort zone to grow yourself and your teams.*

I call this segment of coaching "Recalibrate for Results™ " because it usually requires leaders and their teams to step back and take a truly honest look at how they function—the good, the bad, and the ugly: how the business functions, how the decisions get made, how the action steps get chosen, and whether there's follow-through in a way that's expected or anticipated. What gets in the way of staying aligned as you navigate unexpected obstacles or opportunities? What's in place that will help you stay aligned? What's already working?

Designing Intentional Alignment

Productivity combines energy (the effort required), effectiveness (producing a quality outcome), and efficiency (use of time) based on decisions that were made with accurate information.

Busy leaders tend to skip over alignment because "it doesn't apply to them," or "it can't possibly be that hard to do," or "that big of a deal," or "it's just not possible that my company wouldn't be internally aligned." Love your optimism. Truly I do. But it's happening in your business, too. How do I know? Because a group of humans work there, and we all have our own ideas and ways of doing things that don't necessarily line up with other people.

Some of you are nodding your head because you've already lived through the cost of misalignment. And you felt the "Seriously????" moment when you discovered the root cause of it because it can be simple steps to fix it. The hard part is being consistent and not budging an inch when there's an opportunity to skip some steps because "you're busy" or "they're busy." Sound familiar?

Steps to Design Intentional Alignment:

1. Shared Purpose – You might call this the Vision or Mission of the company.

"Shared," meaning you've conveyed it to the teams, vendors, suppliers, stakeholders, board, customers, or shareholders if you're not a privately held company. As you may already know, a stakeholder is anyone with a "stake" in what you are planning, meaning someone who will be impacted directly or indirectly by what you're about to do.

If you've done any PR (public relations) in your career, you realize that a purpose that connects to your product/service or is important to you and your people is what helps your business stand out. It makes it human for your clients, customers, and employees. And for you. This is the purpose for the existence of your business, which you, as a leader, share with your teams.

2. Stated Goals – Don't assume that you and your teams are on the same page about "what's obvious" that needs to be addressed or accomplished to live the purpose and create the priorities. State the goals out loud and write them down.

3. Clear Priorities – These are the result of the Shared Purpose and Stated Goals and are not separate from them. Clients always have more on the list to achieve than is possible in whatever time frame they have defined. Priorities are where you select which items directly produce those goals in service of that Shared Purpose.

4. Growth Action Plans – These might be project management plans, project plans, or an action step outline—something that shows you have thought through what it's going to take to implement the selected priorities connected to the goals, and show you are living the purpose of the business. Identify the dependencies between resources and teams here.

5. People Needs – Recognize that *none* of the work happens without you, the leader, *and* the teams you lead. None of it. An often-overlooked element of alignment is what the employees need and the team dynamics in the business.

The people dynamics are the undercurrent of how you function as an organization, whether you consciously realize it or not. It's why I covered teamwork in the prior chapter. Developing high-performing teams of people who feel safe to ask questions, be questioned, make mistakes, celebrate success, and even laugh at work is part of what makes alignment sustainable. Things will and do change. The dynamics of how you work together define whether those changes will be horribly painful or merely annoying. Or if they are even noticed as a problem. They may even be embraced!

Why do I include the people items *after* the business items? Because the people items need context. If we begin with the people's needs, we would be discussing topics like employee satisfaction, fulfillment, reaching their full potential, hiring those who want to be lifelong learners, and people who are team players. All of these are important; however, without the business items discussion first, they don't have any context. *It's what your business does as a purpose that provides the context for what the people who want to work there contribute to the company and to the purpose of the company.* By the way, the people needs include yours too, executive leader. You are one of the people, too, though often you are overlooked in these discussions. Just pausing for a moment to say to you, "I see you" and "I know you have needs too."

So, in using my method for alignment, we discuss the business items first. Then, we examine what the people need to achieve those goals. What resources will be required? What adjustments will need to be made to existing priorities? What learning will need to be developed? What changes will be critical to move obstacles out of the way? What expansion of skills and strengths will become essential to fulfill that purpose? And the pivotal questions: How do we function now that will serve us during these changes? How do we function now that will interfere?

Keys to Success

Often, I see companies use these different components of alignment; they just use them backward, which is why they don't work. And why it's so costly in terms of rework, wasted effort, and energy spent dealing with stressful situations that were *entirely preventable*.

Busy teams, busy employees, and busy leaders can make snap judgments and take action before discussing and defining what is to be achieved or resolved. So, you quickly get to work assuming "everyone already knows what's going on."

They don't. And neither do you as the leader.

Alignment is created when you use the components in the correct order: Shared Purpose, Stated Goals, Clear Priorities, Growth Action Plans, and People Needs. This is how you maximize productivity and reduce rework. Do this for **all** decisions, not just the easy ones, the strategic ones, or the ones you "have time" to think about.

Use the goal as the filter for decisions. Decisions are made, and actions are taken that directly connect with the goals, not function outside of the goals. If you are committed to eating more nutritious food, then use that goal as the filter for the choices you make at each meal. Without having the goal front and center, it's like you don't have the goal at all, and you haven't defined priorities for the actions you take that relate to that goal. What that really says is, "I'm saying I want to eat better, but I'm not that committed to doing it." Just to be clear, I'm not a health coach. No judgment here for what you eat. Personally, I like vegetables. I also like dessert and bacon. So, I'm just sharing an example.

Here's another example: If your goal is for your teams to collaborate better, but you continue to cancel team meetings, how do you expect the collaboration to change? Yes, there's a lot to consider in how you guide your team to become better at collaboration—that's true. So, what are those steps? If you use the goal of improving collaboration as the filter for your decisions and resulting actions, what steps would you take today?

I'm not saying you aren't busy or pressed for time. I'm saying your priorities are not matching your goals, which means the effort you are using is likely producing results you don't want or incomplete results that leave you scratching your head.

Resist the urge to simply feel like you're making progress because you are "doing things" without actually knowing if what you are doing will lead you to where you want to go or create the business results you're trying to achieve.

Instead, step back. Pause. This doesn't have to take a long time to do. Consider what the situation is right now and what you want it to be instead, then define those goals. Now, prioritize the pieces to do first, second, etc. Then, define the actions to take based on the measures of success you've identified. These are the measures that will tell you if this effort is working toward the goal. Now, you need the leadership abilities that are taught throughout this book to ensure it's sustainable.

In order to gain alignment, you must first correct the misalignment.

Correcting the Misalignment

The first step to correcting the misalignment is giving a voice to the invisible. Instead of ignoring what is really happening—the rush to act, the hurry to complete without the needed information, the murky and mushy goals—be willing to say it out loud to your team. Own your role in creating these confusing conditions as the leader.

You might be surprised at the exhale that happens in your teams, even if you're all virtual. Someone might even say, "*finally*," because they've been waiting for this to be addressed, but they didn't feel like they could do it because "that's just how things are." Yikes.

If this doesn't resonate with you because your teams do question and speak up, great! Still, pause and consider if they speak up on "safe" topics only. Are they willing to dig into difficult subjects that might feel confrontational or cause a rift in the team? If you're nodding, it's okay. Now you know and can begin to shift how the dynamics function by changing how you lead yourself and how you lead them.

In one client's situation, the owner was frustrated by the stagnation in revenue in their professional service business. While he had an established business, he could see that the business had more potential for delivering services. He couldn't determine the bottlenecks stopping him from unleashing it. They had smart and dedicated staff. They had a great sales pipeline based on a specialized niche in their industry. However, their clients waited up to two months for services, which was costing them cash flow, and the customers needed help with more urgent solutions.

After working with the four-person leadership team and the owner, I learned more about how this owner led his team. He was having team meetings, but he did all the talking, so it was mostly a one-way exchange. He did have a sales process but made a lot of assumptions about what his team understood about business development. The quality of their work was unmatched in their industry, and their clients were very complimentary about their experience. The goal of growing revenue had been conveyed, but no one could determine what was causing the blocks to raising it. So, what were the problems?

You might have already picked up on the fact that they had a training gap and a communication gap. Both were blind spots to the owner and leadership team. When we corrected the training gap in the receptionist, she was able to direct the client requests to the correct paths. People seeking information were directed to their free education classes, as they should be, and not consuming an appointment on the schedule. That meant the appointments were available for those clients with urgent situations who were more immediate buyers. As a result, their average monthly revenue went up by 44 percent in the first year of our work together.

It sounds so simple, right? That's easy to say when you are on the outside of the situation. Living inside the business makes it harder to see your own blind spots on your own. It's part of being human. I'm a coach, and I have a coach for this same reason.

Blind Spots That Interfere with Alignment

Reactive Distractions

Without alignment in your goals and effort, every day is a volatile blur, and it's not clear what you actually accomplished. Erratic choices without sound business wisdom create chaos or even stagnation while people try to figure out "what's really going on."

What happens when you solve this blind spot? Empowered Focus. Because now, you and your teams know what to do, when, and *why* through mutually understood goals. Productivity soars as everyone gets on the same page. How to stay there is outlined in the next chapter.

Team Conflict in Problem-Solving

How people examine the business conditions in a situation, evaluate a scenario, or identify issues, obstacles, and opportunities are often different. For example, consider what you learned about your thinking patterns when you reviewed the *Effective Versus Efficient Self-Awareness Exercise* from Chapter 4.

Another challenge in problem-solving comes when the tolerance for analysis differs among teammates. Quick action-takers need little information. Detail-oriented leaders want all the information possible. Quick people miss critical details, which causes problems later. Analytical people push deadlines because they aren't ready to declare anything.

What I often see are teams that are having entirely different conversations about what they think is the same problem but isn't. It stems from their differing viewpoints of what is actually the problem and what is actually causing the problem. And the fact that they assume that everyone thinks like they do.

When this blind spot is resolved, efficiency soars. When you get on the same page about the problem you are solving, your time invested in implementing the solution is optimized.

Sticky Situations

Leading diverse teams can be a tricky situation for any leader. Creating alignment in direction and goals with a group of people with different levels of experience, backgrounds, education, thought processes, years at the company, and different generations can be overwhelming for the leader. If this struck a nerve, take a breath. If you have experience with this already, lean into what you've already learned.

It's not possible to keep everyone happy all the time.

It's not possible to be liked by everyone all the time.

It is possible to lead everyone all the time.

The stark difference between leading them and having a goal of keeping them happy is the outcome you are aiming for. Yes, be personable and relatable. Yes, genuinely care about each person on your team individually and as a group. Both of these actions will go a long way in building mutual respect. At the end of the day, respecting each other's similarities and differences is what will drive honest and frank conversation where everyone feels heard, whether or not they agree with each other or with you.

This is what you need when leading diverse teams: mutual respect built by being heard, openly being able to share your ideas and concerns, and an agreement in the Team Charter and Shared Commitments as to how you function (see Chapter 4).

Decisions will be made, and not everyone will agree with them. Nonetheless, you will move ahead together. Alignment is the solution to Recalibrate for Results™. Communication is the fastest avenue to create alignment. This business-critical element is discussed in the next chapter.

CHAPTER 7
OPTIMIZE COMMUNICATION
PIVOTAL PRINCIPLE FOR LEADING DELIBERATE GROWTH® #4

Better communication is the fastest way to improve efficiency in any business.

Let's start with why we must focus on communication in the first place. Investing in better communication is the fastest way to improve efficiency in any business. Communication is the key to increased effectiveness in business and in relationships.

You might analyze something by yourself at your desk as you ponder different options, and then you must communicate with someone else for those options to become a reality. For those options to be analyzed from other perspectives, and to explore ideas you hadn't thought about yet.

Whether you communicate well or not, communication is the method to move work through the business. From bringing in new customers or clients to fulfilling orders and delivering services and from managing suppliers and vendors to navigating changing conditions in the industry, or just choosing how to respond to the unexpected.

Yes, you can think by yourself. Then, what you think about and the conclusions that you draw need to be conveyed to someone else. That's communication. It's the most overlooked advantage any leader has and the most underleveraged ability leaders use. And it's the least prioritized skill developed in teams. Why? Because people assume that because everyone communicates, everyone knows how to do it well.

You know that's not true. You've been in situations where "That's not what I meant!" escaped your lips. Or "What are you talking about?" Or "How did you come up with that as the goal I was talking about?"

On the other hand, good communication can result in "That's exactly what I was talking about!" demonstrating a confirmation and shared understanding of your intended meaning. We all celebrate when that happens! We assume that happens all the time in each interaction. It doesn't. But we think it does. Oops.

What Communication Really Is

Communication is not really about communicating. It's about how *information flows* through the business. Information like industry changes, strategic priorities, business goals, status updates, new initiatives, changes in priorities, people changes, social events, community contributions, success stories, urgent problems, client/customer information, product or service changes, technology opportunities or challenges, and new business directions.

How you prevent rework and uncover duplication of work is by having clear communication and honest conversations. In my experience, it is not usually the process itself that is the issue; it's the *use* of the process. Meaning, it's how people go about their jobs to implement their piece of the process and how they interact with their teams or colleagues to do so. That is a communication problem, an information flow problem, not a process problem. The steps are known in the process; they just aren't being implemented well.

Just this week, a client uncovered a problem with duplication of work. The second-generation owner had a plan for product development, and the product development manager had a different plan. The workflow defined who did what, but given they didn't talk with each other—aka lack of communication and information flow—the product ended up at a supplier for unnecessary modifications. Thankfully, they discovered this mistake and could retrieve those products before any changes were made.

"So, what's the big deal?" you might be wondering. It was caught in time, so you just move on, right? Well, let's do the math. It cost the product development manager half a day of time delivering and then retrieving the parts. It cost the owner two hours of stress and frustration rerouting the solution. That's six hours of time lost because of correcting something that was **entirely preventable**. Both people thought they were doing the best thing for the business at the time. Neither considered otherwise. Both were shocked when their duplication was discovered and a little speechless that it happened.

This is where people chalk things up to "it was just a misunderstanding." On the surface, that's true. Let's look deeper. How often does this happen with your team? Across your teams? Within your business? With your clients or customers? Or suppliers or vendors? Or other stakeholders? These scenarios are entirely preventable when the focus is put on the right things. In this situation, the miscommunication was created by an assumption about who does what and *why*. And it caused six hours of rework to correct it.

The next cost to consider is what they could have been doing in those six hours instead. Working on the next PO? Engaging with a new client? Creating a new product idea? Serving an existing client or customer? Holding the team meeting that was canceled? It's not just the cost of correcting the mistake to consider. It's the *opportunity cost* of how that time could have been spent more productively without the lack of communication. Did you catch that strain on productivity? This example only involves two of the people in the business. Now multiply that cost across your company.

Rework is an expensive, time-draining, and energy-sucking hole. It's caused by poor communication within a team or between teams, or maybe with vendors or suppliers outside the business, or even with your customer or client because you didn't ask enough questions to really get an understanding of their goals, needs, or requirements.

Communication encompasses all the pieces I've discussed so far in this book and is why I've stressed the importance of going through the *Pivotal Principles for Leading Deliberate Growth®* in order: leading instead of reacting using a Growth Mindset, learning to lead for growth through teamwork, and creating alignment so that the results you desire are what actually happens. How those principles come to life is through the use of communication. How you deal with conflict is based on how you can communicate with others while maintaining a Growth Mindset and teamwork attitude.

Requirements for ~~Communication~~ Information Flow

Leading by Example

When leaders prioritize communication and understand its nuances in information flow, the whole business runs more smoothly. Caring about communication **demonstrates** a leader's commitment to creating mutual understanding with others. It sets an example for your leadership team and your employees that sharing information and staying on the same page is an expectation of how things run at your company.

Even experienced leaders like you can have dips in energy. You're tired. You've been dealing with that arduous issue that's been frustrating you for weeks. You can't imagine having that employee meeting in the middle of this because you just aren't feeling up for it.

I get it. You're human too.

Just like you would expect from your teams, it's important to muster the energy to do your *entire* job, not just the parts happening right now or the parts that you like the best. Some of this is learning to manage your energy, and some of this goes back to your mindset, your view of yourself and your role in the organization, and how you prioritize information flow. As I have said before, you have information that is different from what your teams have, and they need what you know to do their jobs in the best way possible.

Business Knowledge

Everyone in the business makes decisions every day with every conversation, email, text, or meeting. What are those decisions based on??? The business knowledge they have at the time of the decision, including the latest change you might have made as the executive leader or even what you've decided to keep the same. If your team doesn't know what you've decided to keep the same and what you've decided to change at any given point, they are making decisions based on old information. Uh-Oh. Hence, information flow is critical for building efficiency in a business so that the decisions each person makes as they do their job are the best possible choices they can make.

To do their job well, team members must possess knowledge about the goals of the business, company vision and mission, and an understanding of how each person's role contributes to that purpose, especially their own. It forms the basis of information for all decisions and includes the technical skills and knowledge specific to your industry, plus what's needed for each person's role.

Business knowledge also includes tracking any metrics used to measure the progress and performance of the business, the teams, and even each individual. How this information is shared depends upon the context of the measurement. (Of course, individual measurements are only to be known by that person and are part of that employee's professional development plan.)

Key performance indicators (KPIs) are often organization-wide, like profitability, service levels, or employee satisfaction, and are shared across the business. Note that measures across the company are usually outcomes, not progress measures. Profitability is a result of progress measures like growing margins or managing expenses. Service levels are the result of the elements of service defined with that client or customer, like responsiveness, meeting deadlines, delivering to client requirements, or managing scope. Measurement creates focus, so measure what you want to move.

Communication Method

This might also be known as a communication channel like email, phone calls, video meetings, text, chat, DM, video calls, and company communication avenues like an intranet, all employee meetings, message boards, team meetings, and one-on-one communication.

Communication Skills

For information flow, essential abilities to deliver the message include adapting to the audience, asking questions, being questioned, limiting assumptions, being responsive, creating connection, effective listening, conflict management, and proactively speaking up.

Listening is the number one underused communication skill, but it has *the most impact* on creating an effective exchange of *meaningful information based on a mutual understanding*. I'll share more on developing your listening aptitude later in this chapter.

Communication skills also include understanding the nuances of body language, facial expressions, gestures, and even the use of emojis. "Reading the room" is part of a communication skill that combines the non-verbal signs of the people with the energy in the room or how the room feels.

Your Mindset About Communication

How you think about communication directly impacts how effective you are when you are doing it. Is communication essential? Is it just something that happens? Is it intentional? Do you invest time in considering it?

Leaders who prioritize communication skills for themselves and others experience a lot less stress from misunderstandings and those dumbfounded moments when you wonder, "How on earth did that just happen??"

If communication is just a thing that happens, your team will also approach it that way. If they try to prioritize improving communication but are met with resistance from you, at some point, they will give up.

The employees you want to keep will leave from sheer exhaustion. The ones you would be okay with leaving will stay because they can hide their lackluster performance behind poor communication.

When you choose to make communication skills a priority, you will become a better leader. One creates the other. By the same token, if communication is an afterthought, you will struggle to be heard, to be understood, and to be followed as a leader.

Structure for Information Flow

The most efficient way to get on the same page, and stay on the same page, is by leveraging what I have named the *Automatic Avenues of Accountability*. These are tools used to create alignment with structures used to enable information flow. These are those weekly team meetings, project status conversations, department meetings, strategic planning meetings, business unit updates, company meetings, employee meetings, putting-out-fires discussions, staff meetings, and strategic retreats.

How do these structures create accountability? They are visible avenues of communication. Within these avenues, people are asked questions about the status of their work as part of the group discussion, so there's nowhere to hide if they've fallen behind, and there's a group celebration when projects are going well. It works both ways!

When you learn how to lead these Automatic Avenues of Accountability effectively, you'll discover the depth and breadth of the advantage they can create. For example, learn to craft the message you want to convey and consider what you want to learn from the group, as well as what the group can learn from each other. You could also discover unknown problems or opportunities and develop the resulting conclusions or decisions. It might be that you reveal the strategic next steps or even a clear path of action to take. Remember that it's not all up to you, leader. These structures should be designed to create conversation, innovation, problem-solving, and solutions that are developed by the team.

The owner of an established small business of forty-five people met with a five-person leadership team daily. Yep, daily. The structure was in place, but the content was not. The intention of this client was good, but the implementation was incomplete. It was more of an exercise in "we're supposed to do this" instead of "what are we doing this for?" No one was invested in the process, and usually, people arrived late and unprepared.

Through our work together, this owner's confidence to question his team and be questioned by his team grew exponentially. He realized that gathering people daily was the right structure to have, but many changes needed to be made to maximize the time invested in that structure. He agreed to ask for feedback from his leadership team about what information exchange would be beneficial to them in those daily discussions.

He was quite surprised with their answers since very little information that they needed was actually being discussed. They left those meetings and still had to look up the information they needed to make decisions that day about their department. It explained a lot about why people didn't value those meetings. It was also telling that no one spoke up to say anything.

The owner had no idea that this was the dynamic happening in his leadership team. It was a big blind spot for him that the daily meetings, which were the right thing to do, were so ineffective. And, as he admitted, it didn't occur to him to ask his team what they needed. In his mind, it was his job to provide the information and their job to consume it. Now, if you had asked this leader whether he was running a one-way communication business, he would have been offended at the notion, except, unknowingly, he was doing just that. Let yourself off the hook if part of this feels a little familiar. Now that you have more awareness, you can change your approach.

Here's the thing. Changing the purpose of those discussions to be much more comprehensive didn't take a lot more time. About fifteen minutes was all. That fifteen minutes saved each person an hour or more during the day, netting them a forty-five-minute gain *every day*. That's

3.75 hours per week *per person*, which is nearly a half day of work based on an eight-hour workday!

The ripple effect of better information exchanges during those daily meeting interactions soaked into how this leadership team interacted with each other outside of those meetings. What developed was more comfort in questioning each other and less emotional stress when someone was the one being questioned.

If this story didn't resonate with you, hooray! Still take the learning parts to ask more questions of your team. You'll be surprised what you uncover that you were assuming was "fine" or "working well." Your people have ideas they haven't yet voiced because there hasn't been an opportunity to do so, or they haven't seen an opening to create that opportunity.

Make it easier for your teams to come to you with their innovative ideas. Create a structure for discussion where new ideas are heard. You could even make that the sole purpose of a meeting and hold it quarterly, semi-annually, or more often, depending upon the pace of your business.

Sticky Situations

Finding Your Voice

When you or your teams are frustrated because you've tried things that aren't working, it's easy to lose hope. In a culture of Fixed Mindset people with Limiting Beliefs, this means people stop trying. They become silent. They figure no one cares anyway, so why bother? They start to internalize the "failure" of whatever they are working on and withdraw.

You'll notice they stop sharing ideas. The team stops talking with each other, or it becomes a little too polite. Team meetings conclude a little too quickly, with a lot of chatter after the meeting that didn't happen during the meeting.

These are warning signs that people have lost their voice and stop speaking up. They don't believe you want to hear what they have to say because, in their mind, you stopped listening. You don't value their expertise or their experience anymore.

Ask yourself a tough question: Have you disappeared? Have you stopped having regular communication with this team or teams? Did you not follow up on something that didn't quite work as intended? Were you dismissive of a big project they pulled off, and it seemed like you didn't even notice?

That might sting a little if it feels familiar. It's okay to be human. It's okay to be a developing leader. It's even okay to admit when you've made a mistake. It's actually the first step to repair this situation and help your team find their voice again.

If it feels like you're the one who lost your voice, you're in good company. Nearly all my one-on-one coaching clients have a dimension of this issue for themselves. Somehow, they have forgotten their own value and what it means to lead. Remember my client who had 325 people reporting up through her who saved the business $800,000 with one decision? She didn't need more technical knowledge about how to do her job. She needed to reconnect with her own value, incorporate a new viewpoint of her role as a leader, and understand the resulting impact of how she led. She found her voice again and leaned into being a growth-minded CEO.

Getting Answers When You Need Them

You already know that even as the executive leader or owner of the business, you don't have all the answers, nor could you possibly know everything that is happening in the company. It's not possible, nor is it necessary, when you've built teamwork that's a verb. So, information flow is interdependent. You have information that your teams need, and they have information that you need. Trust and communication are a two-way street. You want them to keep you up to date on changing conditions that impact deadlines, service delivery, production schedules, and expenses.

So, if you are working on something and need to go get some answers, approach your employee as a team member yourself. Approaching with the demeanor of "the boss" comes with expectations, whether we like it or not. Seek the information merely as a fellow team member. When you delve into an issue as a fellow problem-solver, it means you are participating in the process and not derailing it because the boss is now involved. How effective this exchange is depends on the trust built within the team and with you.

The Round-Robin Email

Ah, the round-robin email with ten people on it. It's dreaded by all who receive it. By the time you've seen the third person responding, that's it. People are not digging back far enough to hear everyone's perspective. People aren't reading it. And neither are you, I would guess. Schedule a meeting.

With a skillfully facilitated meeting, you can handle this conversation in a few minutes. Yes, scheduling is one of the challenges for this objective. I get that. It's one of the reasons that someone sent an email instead.

So, get creative about scheduling for this particular topic. Is this a repetitive issue? Does this need to be included in the agenda of an already-standing meeting? Is this issue causing a fire right now that really needs to be prioritized instead of pushed off into an email for when people "get to it?"

Think in terms of the information flow and people needing to make decisions about their own work. What will actually provide information so that your people can make smart decisions and take effective action? A round-robin email sounds like a good idea, but it isn't.

Still stuck on round-robin emails? Then establish Ground Rules for reading them—the whole thing. Still, it won't work all the time, and people will miss things. And since there's no tone of voice in written communication, people read it according to what they assume the person meant or based on their own tone of voice. It's still very risky for conveying accurate information. Meet.

The Key Person Missed the Meeting

So, what if you do meet, and the key person that you most needed to attend wasn't there? Did the person who missed the conversation delegate attendance to anyone else? You're the executive leader, yet you know that doesn't substitute for the expertise of your people. You have subject matter experts on your team who are there for a reason.

What made them a key person for this topic or this decision? Who else is involved with that issue? Was that person in attendance? Has everyone involved been informed? Notice the tracking of information flow that is needed to figure all of this out.

If they did designate someone else to attend for them, that person doesn't have the same ideas as the key person. Of course not. We're all different. Now we've crossed into an area where communication meets authority meets delegation meets "Who is in charge anyway?"

So, you tried to create information flow, and it was met with interference because your SME (subject matter expert) wasn't available. What made you schedule the conversation at a time when they weren't available? Or did they have a personal emergency that popped up? Why did you hold the meeting anyway? Usually, it's because it's difficult to get people's calendars together or you have a tight deadline to meet.

The question becomes, "What are you going to do about it now that it already happened?" When you led the discussion, even without your SME, were people participating in the discussion or mostly waiting to defer to the SME when they returned to the office? If you have built teamwork that includes the ability to question each other, including questioning the SME, there should have been a lively discussion even without them. You might even uncover ideas you wouldn't have otherwise because the SME would have done all the talking.

Hmmm ... it sounds like their absence might have created a brainstorming opportunity—a chance for other voices to speak up and be heard. Use this opportunity to notice the ideas that surface. Take the list to the SME when they return and review the discussion. You might need to schedule a follow-up discussion to ensure people are on the same page. At the very least, send a summary email outlining the key points of the conversation.

You're Stuck Waiting on Someone Else

I previously mentioned the interdependence of teams on each other. Within the team and between teams, what each person does or doesn't do impacts someone else on their team or on another team.

How do you get yourself out of that? Your project is probably stalled. Although, as the executive leader, this doesn't happen to you as much. You can always pull rank and get what you need. Be careful of doing that too much because you won't be seen as a team player anymore— just a dictator boss running amuck again.

The most effective way to approach this scenario is with careful communication. Be very clear about the information that you are waiting on, and double-check who you believe has the answers you need.

5 Ingredients for Unlocking Effective Communication

Because communication is a linchpin of productivity and efficiency, I developed a model to outline the key steps. It applies to all communication methods, written or verbal.

1. Define the Purpose

What is the intention and desired result of the communication? As Stephen Covey taught me years ago in *The 7 Habits of Highly Effective People*, "Begin with the End in Mind." Also, consider who really needs to be part of the questions and the answers. Identify the time frame and check your attitude about this topic.[5]

---

5   Covey, Stephen. In *7 Habits of Highly Effective People Companion Workbook*, 50. Accessed 1996.

5 INGREDIENTS FOR UNLOCKING EFFECTIVE COMMUNICATION				
1. DEFINE THE PURPOSE	**2. RECOGNIZE YOUR FILTER**	**3. DEVELOP THE MESSAGE**	**4. LISTEN AND RECEIVE**	**5. FOLLOW THROUGH**
• Intention and Desired Result • Attitude and Energy • Who is Involved • Timeframe and Urgency	• Assumptions About the Situation and Others • Beliefs About Yourself • Filter is Always in Use	• Delivery Method • How You Say or Write It Matters • Confirm Who is Receiving It	• Be Fully Present in THIS Exchange • What Could You Ask Versus What Do You Want to Say	• Connect the Discussion With Next Steps • Create Productive Not Wasteful Impact

When successfully applied, these five ingredients create the keys to unlocking productive communication for yourself and within your company, regardless of your role.

© Copyright 2025 Center for Deliberate Growth®

2. Recognize Your Filter

Everyone has a bias, which I also call a filter because of how it filters your experience of something. This is the context for how you communicate and directly influences your outcomes.

A bias creates assumptions about the people involved and the situation. You might also have beliefs about yourself that interfere with how you are leading this scenario. Those could be helping or hurting the situation for you, depending on how they impact the way you show up. What's the energy and attitude you have when you arrive, make the call, or start the conversation? Are you in your Growth Mindset or Fixed Mindset? Note that your filter, aka your bias, is always in use. The more you know yourself and learn your own bias, the more effective your communication will become as you open your mind to listening more effectively to others.

3. Develop the Message and Choose the Method

How you say it matters, and know that written communication is different than verbal. Written communication doesn't come with any tone of voice or body language. It's why someone invented emojis for text messages and why they are so heavily used. We humans need the emotional context for a text message. Be aware of how you write and speak and how that might be received by the person you are communicating with. Be especially mindful when writing business emails, given that the use of emojis is generally less acceptable.

Develop the message based on the person receiving the information, not on how you would like to receive it or stated in a way that you would understand. You're not sending this to yourself.

What communication method will you use to deliver your message? In person? Video? Email? Text? DM? Phone call? Choose the avenue that will allow for the best information exchange. If they are waiting on information from you, then an email might be sufficient. If you need information from them, the initial request might be sent by email, though they may have questions about your request that are best explored in a conversation over the phone or video. Texting or DMs are a dangerous choice. People abbreviate what they mean and think others know what they are talking about.

Some of my clients have kids or grandkids in high school who use all sorts of interesting texting abbreviations. In one instance, I received an email from a CEO client that included those abbreviations like they forgot they weren't talking with their kids. This is a very specific example of not being in alignment with yourself. Their purpose was to send me a question about a business issue they were working on, but what they sent me was an email full of abbreviations that I didn't know how to decipher. We laughed a lot about that message, and it certainly served as a lesson for both of us. I learned more about high school texting language, and my business owner client learned how important it is to take a step back, pause, and then send an email.

4. Listen and Receive

I'm saying it again: Listening is the number one underused communication skill, yet it has the most impact on creating a meaningful exchange. Period. Listening, not talking, is leading. How?

Better listening changes the interaction for the better! We are in such a hurry that we listen to see if we're right instead of listening to what the person is actually saying. We're listening to see if our assumptions are true, but still not listening to what the person is saying. We're formulating what we're going to say instead of paying attention to what they are saying. Yikes.

Be fully present for *this* exchange of information without assumptions about the content of the conversation. Listen with your heart and soul, not just your head. You're having an exchange with another person, not a robot. Take a genuine interest in this person and their perspective.

Consider what you could ask instead of focusing on what you want to say. Be curious to learn the other person's perspective and viewpoint. Ask more questions than you talk. Ask to learn information, deepen your understanding, clarify what they meant, or brainstorm new information.

Yes, you can share your thoughts and expertise too. If they wish to participate in a two-way exchange of meaningful information, they will be asking you questions as well. Listen to the question being asked, not the one you assume they meant. If you aren't sure what they are asking, then ask about that. And don't make people guess what you mean. That's just passive-aggressive, time-wasting emotional stress for both of you. Create Shared Agreements or Ground Rules in your team, where being direct is part of how you function.

If you're not accustomed to being direct, and that feels very uncomfortable to you, let that be okay. It's a growth edge for you, an area of professional development for you to focus on. For those of us who are already direct, be aware that there is a line where *too direct* can happen. Be "kindly honest," as I call it. Have some tact in your approach, but don't make the person guess what you mean. Say what you mean with some awareness about the person (or group) you are communicating with at the time. These are mindsets and abilities that I coach leaders to develop, and as a result, they create more efficiency in how the business is run.

5. Follow Through

Connect the exchange of information with next steps. What was decided? What's still pending? Did you have the information that you needed, or is there more to explore before you can make the next decision? Write down the follow-up steps in a summary email. Add them to the project plan, if there is one, or the Growth Action Plan. Don't rely on your memory or theirs to know what was discussed and who is going to do what. I guarantee that people will remember it differently, so at the conclusion of each meeting or exchange, pause a moment to clarify the decisions made, the action steps to be taken, and who is doing them. Yep, it's direct accountability in front of everyone. High-performing teams like the clarity of this step. If your team hides from this, explore why that is. Something within their interactive dynamics is making them feel unsafe setting clear expectations.

What if you don't agree? Conflict will happen. It's a given. But it doesn't have to be a bad thing or feel terrible or hurt people's feelings. It could just be that you have differing viewpoints about the problem you are solving or how to solve it. An often-overlooked communication skill is facilitation, the ability to navigate a discussion with a group of people who have diverse opinions. Even if everyone thinks the same, conflict can arise down the line as a result of someone daring to disagree because "that never happens."

It's why the summary of the discussion is so essential. If those who disagree haven't spoken up yet, they might when the decision is about to be made that they have a differing idea about. Your job as the facilitator of the discussion is to uncover these differences before the end of the meeting. Why? Because that happened at the end and just extended the conversation another thirty minutes.

Dig into diverse opinions earlier in the meeting so that when you get to the concluding point, it can actually be a concluding point. That doesn't mean that you've stopped discussions on the topic because you might not be done yet. What it means is that you've concluded some things and have some open items yet to be explored, which usually means that you'll be having another meeting. Don't groan—I heard that. I don't have a magic potion to prevent the next meeting from happening. Instead, embrace that it's actually a good thing to have clarity on the status of the issue you are exploring and everyone on the same page about the next steps.

A key pivot point of communication lives in that clarity. Hands down, meetings are one of the most efficient and effective modes of communication, period. People hate them because they aren't run very well. One big skill gap is the skill of facilitation—that is what you are using when you lead a meeting. It's the art of listening, asking questions, navigating the interactions and dynamics of the group, and understanding the business issues combined with the fortitude to create an outcome for the group.

Why do I have such a soap box about meetings? Because they are easier to make effective than people realize. An agenda isn't enough. Start with the purpose of the meeting. Are you there to decide something, explore something, fix something, teach something, learn something, or develop something? That alone can help determine who needs to be included. Set expectations for people to show up to the meeting prepared with XYZ—you can include that expectation in your Team Charter or your Organizational Commitments for the whole business. Have someone lead the discussion who can facilitate differing ideas and navigate situations when someone shows up unprepared. When you conclude the meeting, voice a summary of what was explored, decided, or opened and the next steps. People hate meetings because these steps aren't done well or aren't done at all. I coach clients about their communication blind spots and developing their expertise to lead effective meetings.

Communication Blind Spots

Message Doesn't Motivate Desired Results
After a talk at a conference, I received an email from the CEO of a medium-sized service business, who became my client. It read: "Weekly, we'll share results with the whole office. Accountability within the calling tree will be in the public nature of internal distribution. If you don't make the calls or document steps, the world will know."

As I reflected on this message and attempt at motivation, its energy said, "individual accountability with a *threat* of accusations and embarrassment if the calls aren't being made or made correctly." While I completely agree with accountability, one of the goals this leader shared with me was how to create more proactive teamwork toward accomplishing the business goals. With that in mind, my recommendation was to shift the energy and mindset around this accountability into building the company and growing the company—*together*. The first step is always to focus on the business goals. In this case, those goals were recently discussed at their company conference.

This approach doesn't mean individual accountability is removed, the contrary, actually. It changes how people *feel* about what they are accomplishing because they align with its purpose. As a result, *their performance will improve*. Instead of "this is your job, so just do it" or "you'll be embarrassed and shamed if you don't," which is leading with fear, intimidation, and control, the energy becomes "the company is on a path to growth, and your role is critical to get us there," which is leading with appreciation, defined expectations, and empowerment.

Now, when this leader reviews the call reports, people are still accountable, and the energy from him is about building the business and not accusing their team of not doing their job. What will happen over time is they will hold each other accountable as a group since that intention is focused on productivity based in a mindset of "we're in this together, and everyone needs to do their part."

Use my *5 Ingredients for Unlocking Effective Communication* above to help yourself align the intention of your message with the right motivation to create the outcome.

Drive-Thru Leadership

In their rush, leaders think there's no need or time to explain anything because everyone should know what they mean and just "get to work." Draining rework and wasted resources result since expectations, actions, and measures of success don't match. So much money leaks—and even gushes—out of businesses with this blind spot.

When this blind spot is known and corrected, Aligned Performance lives in the business. Results quicken, and costs reduce as you close the gap between what you intended to happen and what actually happens.

The Solution: 3 Steps to Easier Interactions

As I repeatedly saw the Drive-Thru Leadership blind spot in action, I developed the *3C Core Communication Model* to help. Using this simple model saves time and boosts productivity as each interaction has more clarity in the meaning, message, purpose, and any decisions that were made. These three steps outline how to structure the interaction to more easily create mutual understanding.

This is the 3C Core Communication Model:

1. CONVEY	2. CONNECT	3. CLARIFY
5-Minute Focus	Processing Pause	Inquiry & Info Flow

© Copyright 2025 Center for Deliberate Growth®

1. **Convey**: *Make time* to share the highlights of your request or question. Only do this when you have a few minutes for an entire exchange of information versus dumping the request and running away. Approach this as a two-way exchange, not a dump-and-run.

2. **Connect**: Ask them, "What other information do you need?" Pause for the person to process your request or question and determine their own questions. Do not run off. Stay on the line or at their desk unless they specifically ask you for more time to process the information. Again, start this discussion when you have a few minutes for a complete exchange.

3. **Clarify**: Answer all of their questions during this exchange. It will save you the round-robin emails heading your way afterward. It will also speed up getting on the same page instead of wasting time to figure that out. Realize that if it takes you ten minutes just to share the highlights, it might take more than two minutes for them to dig into the details they need. Clarify what you each understand at the conclusion of this exchange and define how to proceed. It might be that more information and another conversation will be needed, so be prepared and accepting of that fact.

The Value of Clarify

When one leader put the *3C Core Communication Model* into place, he discovered the value of the Clarify step. Let's start from the beginning. During our work together, a manufacturing leader realized that when conversations ended, it was often with different conclusions. This client would leave the discussion thinking one thing, and the other person would leave thinking another. These conversations included those with his leadership peers and direct reports. These discrepancies weren't discovered until after his team member began implementing things in an entirely different way than he expected. Or they were discovered after he gave instructions to other team members and confused his peers with information they were not expecting. This often led to costly rework!

This leader discovered that the Clarify step was missing. When meetings or hallway conversations happened thereafter, he stopped to clarify what he had concluded and then asked the other person or people what they had concluded.

He admitted to me that it felt awkward to ask. He was sure that people would be offended, assuming he thought they were stupid or incapable of a conversation. He discovered that they weren't offended or even fazed by the question. They were glad for the clarity because they didn't want rework, either! Usually, both people were surprised by the differences in what they concluded and so glad they figured it out before taking any action.

When I asked him how much time it took to stop for clarification, he said, "About ten seconds," with a grin. In one example, he learned that they were on totally different pages about what to do next. If he hadn't stopped to clarify, it would have cost about $4,000 in materials, five hours of time sorting out a solution, and a month of waiting on the new materials. Plus, the domino effect on the production schedule. So, it turns out that ten-second pause to clarify is pretty valuable, huh? He laughed, "Yep." It's his new method of mutually communicating information.

My service business clients don't have material cost involved; however, there certainly is wasted time spent on reworking solutions when people draw different conclusions from the same conversation. Plus the likely impact on service delivery and project schedules because you didn't invest a moment to confirm the mutual understanding.

Whatever your feelings are about change, it's happening. You can choose to fear it or worry about it—or you can learn to *create* it deliberately. As leaders, it's far more satisfying to activate change than it is to mindlessly endure it and the havoc it can wreak. That's what's coming up in the next chapter.

CHAPTER 8

ACTIVATE CHANGE

PIVOTAL PRINCIPLE FOR LEADING DELIBERATE GROWTH® #5

*You can change without growing,
but you cannot grow without changing.*

IN MY EXPERIENCE AS A LEADER AND COACHING LEADERS, CHANGE AND growth are two hot topics. Yet, they are often not discussed together or in a way that identifies their interdependent nature. I said the quote above to a client years ago, and he kindly paused and said, "Write that down. Others will need to hear that. It flipped a switch for me and created a reason for change."

What Is in Your Control?

Change is constant. Change is inevitable. Change is fun. Change is agony.

In talking about change, the first thing I usually coach clients to delineate is the difference between what they can control versus what they can't. Stuff you can control is stuff you can change. Stuff you cannot control is not stuff you can change.

When you focus on what you can control, it easily puts your options into perspective. You can easily see that the economy is not something you can control, even if you want to change it. Pricing from your suppliers or vendors might be something you can influence, though not something you have control over. Real estate prices are not something you can control, even though we would like to. Shipping time frames or even whether the internet service works correctly is not something we can control. We can certainly change who we work with, which makes it something we can control based on the vendor choices we make. Notice these are all external to the business. None of these examples are occurring inside the company.

When I ask clients to tell me what they are worried about right now, the list usually begins with items external to the company, such as the economy, supply chain issues, suppliers meeting deadlines, or service providers delivering on what they said. It can consume some leaders to the point that they have big blind spots about what is happening *inside* their own business—scenarios they have absolute control over to make better or prevent from getting worse, yet they aren't doing either because they have a tunnel vision focused on things they cannot control.

This focus comes from having a Fixed Mindset as opposed to a Growth Mindset. Continuously focusing on what you cannot control and being in the mindset and energy of worry and fear will tank the decisions you make every day. Your perspective will always be to protect everything and not grow anything.

Should you protect things? Of course. Risk management comes with being the executive leader. It's part of every job description whether you own the company or lead the company from the highest point.

When you are only focused on managing risk based on factors outside the company, you aren't aware of or actually taking any responsibility for what is happening inside the company. This means your information loop is lopsided because the only information your leadership team and employees will hear from you is about stuff they cannot control either. How does that help them? Or you?

Yes, be informed. I'm not saying stick your head in the sand and ignore the financial markets or economic indicators. I am saying don't obsess about that as if it's the only factor that will create success. I'll outline how to help yourself, your team, and the business, as this chapter continues.

Activate Change Versus Just Get Through It

Often, I hear about change as something you have to endure and "get through." The tendency is to hunker down and figure everything will work itself out somehow without any intervention.

Nothing could be further from the truth.

Sitting back and "enduring change" is taking a Fixed Mindset to a whole new level. And that's not a compliment. It's creating chaos in the business that is being duplicated throughout the organization. As I've mentioned, the leader is either part of the solution or part of the problem. If you are taking a "wait and see" approach to dealing with change . . . what do you think your teams are doing? Do you wonder why completion has waned? Why deadlines are in danger? Why customer service levels seem to be at risk? Because your teams are following your example to "wait and see what happens." It's what you are doing, right? You're functioning in fear of failure. Or fear of making the wrong decision. So, you don't make any decision—but no decision is still a decision.

Decide to focus on what you can control. Choose to understand the business factors that create favorable and unfavorable conditions *inside* the company. Then, make choices and move ahead using the information you gain from staying informed about what is actually happening inside the organization.

What If This Were Possible?

What if you could make change intentional instead of just waiting for it to happen and then hoping you can deal with it? What if you could create it at will? What if your teams would follow you through it? What if it's easier than you think? What if you knew how to maximize the attitude of some of your people who love change instead of running from them because you don't? Or are you the one who loves change, but cannot figure out how to lead others through it? Stay with me. I'm about to share five factors that will help.

Creating More Time to Lead Change: 5 Factors to Lean On

You're always going to be busy. Period. There's not going to be a time when things "slow down" enough that you feel like you have plenty of time to do what you want. And if there is that time, you're going to be figuring out how to "ramp things up again." Right?

The need to lead is constant. You are always leading. In every conversation, email, text, chat message, phone call, and video, you are demonstrating your leadership style and effectiveness. With every decision or lack of decisions—since no decision is a decision—you are demonstrating your priorities and willingness to be uncomfortable.

There will never be enough time to do everything you want to do. That's a fact. So, how do you manage your time? How do you help your team manage their time? Here are five factors that will help you lead change.

1. Time management is not about time. It's about priorities.

Priorities are what is most important or impactful that directly connects to the goals you've defined. If you choose to prioritize something that does not connect to your goals, ask yourself, "Do I have different goals than what I stated? Am I getting distracted by ideas that are cool but not important? Is this a brainstorming thought for a later innovation?" Careful about that last one; it becomes the excuse for many time-consuming distractions for you and your teams.

2. Understand how to get things done through others.

Knowing how to lead others to contribute to the goals you've conveyed is crucial. Developing teamwork as a daily action is one of the keys to achieving this, as I discussed in a prior chapter. *Commit* to understanding how to use teamwork for everyone's benefit.

3. There's one question that leverages your time by solving multiple things at the same time.

It's the question that engages your teams, clarifies priorities, aligns decisions, and identifies action steps simultaneously. This *one* question is: **"Why?"**

Asking "why" is something we humans have done since we were little. Toddlers run around asking why about everything. We never stop wanting the answer to that, though we might stop directly asking the question. Because we still want the answer, it stimulates how we thoughtfully respond or emotionally react to situations or people.

So, instead of making your teams wonder or make up their own answers as they fill in blanks you left out, just answer them. Especially in situations of changing priorities. Especially in scenarios where employee roles are changing. Especially when there's a fire burning with an unhappy client or customer. Especially when you are about to stretch their capacity or their knowledge in ways you've never done before.

Put their minds and their emotions at ease by answering the question "Why?" and answering it up front. If you don't answer it yourself, they will fill in the blanks for themselves while they speculate on the answer. They might spend *hours* discussing it among themselves while they try to determine how this new direction or problem impacts what they are doing right now, tomorrow, or next month. This consumes time you could have saved everyone if you had just answered it up front. Without the clarity from your answer, they will make one up and then make decisions based on this speculation versus actual information from you. Can you hear the rework brewing? I can.

Yes, there are varying degrees of an answer based on the situation. I realize that. Just be transparent. Your teams are going to discuss this whether they are "supposed to" or not. Even high-performing teams are not immune to speculation or even gossip in times of change.

4. Allow time for things to work.

Making one tweak in how you function might be immediately apparent, or it might take some time to take hold. I can coach a leader about their mindset, and it can be readily understood, but it might take time to be absorbed in how it will adjust the leader's thinking and method of operating. The same is true for when you are changing how your team functions, thinks, or makes decisions. We all want results to happen right now! The reality is that results can take some time. Let that be okay.

How does this relate to making time to lead? Because it means you need to include this in the time needed to lead and for outcomes to happen.

5. I'll say this again: Measure what you want to move forward.

Metrics tend to create focused action because people generally respond to something when it's being measured. Be sure you are measuring what actually connects to the change you are creating, aka the goal of the change. Measuring what creates progress versus only measuring the end result is what will create the change you seek. That means you measure activities that lead to the outcome you actually want.

The cross-functional leaders at a tech industry client were struggling to work together despite their best intentions. It turned out everyone wanted things to be better, but they didn't know what to change to break the siloed way they operated to make that possible. As with many leaders, they had their own projects to move forward along with leading their teams. Then their team was responsible for completing work and handing it off to the next team in the process.

The general attitude of this group of leaders was that no one really understood what they did or what their team did, and they just assumed that no one wanted to because no one ever asked them. It just felt like everyone made assumptions from both sides of the equation and silently grumbled, "Why couldn't this be easier?"

What were they missing? Time to lead. Time to develop themselves. Time to consider the actions they were taking and the blind spots that were interfering with their intentions.

Working with me automatically created a structure of development and accountability. Each person recognized blind spots in their thinking, was willing to change how they did things, and listened to the others in the group in ways they hadn't before.

The handoffs between teams became much more efficient as the leaders of those departments started seeking information from each other instead of operating in silent chaos. Their teams relaxed as they had the necessary information to do their jobs the first time. Rework was reduced. They saved two to ten hours per week, according to the self-assessment by this group of nine leaders. That's 2.6 to thirteen work weeks per year based on a forty-hour week *per person*.

What could you be doing with that time? More deeply engaging with your teams. Working on all those strategic ideas you have but never had time to do anything with. Ensuring information flow within and between your teams. Reducing the number of ten- to twelve-hour workdays. Having date night or time with your kids or friends. Having time for yourself.

Blind Spot: Comfort in the Chaos

Despite the desire to grow and improve, you might avoid key decisions to escape the need for change. The turmoil has become "normal," and it's easier to live in it than to figure out how to create more peace for yourself and your teams.

Or you might be numbly stuck in a head-spinning paralysis where you won't do anything because you're afraid to be wrong or you just don't know where to begin.

Building resilience so that you and your teams can function in chaos is not a strength. If it's needed, it tells me that the business is out of alignment, meaning there's confusion about purpose, goals, priorities, effort, information flow, and how each person's role contributes to the business.

You might recall my coaching about alignment in Chapter 6.

What becomes possible when you decide to break up with the chaos?

Deliberate Action. Now, you feel in charge of the business instead of letting the business run over you.

Having the prior executive leader indicted on criminal charges certainly created a different level of chaos for a non-profit client I had. They had been "comfortably" living in a version of chaos for many years, and felt totally blindsided by the criminal choices of their former leader.

The new executive leader walked into a storm of mistrust while people scratched their heads, trying to figure out, "How did we miss that???" This experienced leader engaged me to lead their strategic planning retreat to reboot the business and rebuild trust within the organization and the community.

The executive leader was experienced, though new to this organization. She knew she needed to be able to be fully present and listen during this retreat. She also knew the conversation would be more productive if she could attend as a fellow participant and not as the new leader in charge. This would not have been possible if she tried to lead these strategic discussions herself. She asked me back to facilitate their strategic planning and board retreats for four consecutive years to continue to "shake things up" and "keep us on track," as she said. Their sponsorships increased by 30 percent during that time.

The lesson here is to take time to see the version of change you are experiencing right now. This organization could have controlled many things but didn't. Unfortunately, their former leader created that situation. I'm not saying your business has criminals in it. I'm saying pay attention to the chaos that has become "normal" for you and ask yourself, "What makes this comfortable? Is this really creating results that we want?"

What Motivates People?

Some are motivated by *outcomes*. These people like knowing what to aim for and the ultimate expectation that you have of them. They care about the journey but may not be as detailed as you would like or need them to be. The vision of the result is what excites them. What the result represents excites them. Even the results that could happen thereafter are a motivator.

Some are motivated by the *process* or steps necessary to create that result. These people enjoy figuring out the steps necessary to implement something. They are conscious of the desired result but focus more on how thorough the process has been to produce those results. They are motivated by thinking things through and looking at the scenario from multiple angles. Having a solid process prepared is what motivates them. They want to know that it will work and that it is working to create that result. Their belief centers on: "If the process is sound, the result will happen."

All people are motivated by appreciation, including your leadership team. Teach your leaders to take time to tell people when they are doing good work, and not just when it's great or above and beyond. People need to hear positive feedback even when they are "just doing their job." Otherwise, the only people who get rewarded with appreciation are those who have "hero" opportunities on certain projects. Not everyone has those chances, which means only a fraction of your people will feel appreciated.

Create company structures where appreciation is expressed. These are methods that go beyond the leader merely commenting in a meeting or sending an email. It can be done as the focus of a team meeting or a whole company meeting. Or you can develop an award program where anyone can submit another person for recognition. One of my clients developed this type of program. Any employee, from partner to entry-level employee, can submit someone else for recognition. Those awards are then given out at the company meeting. The partners admit that the use of this system ebbs and flows, but when people are really encouraged to use it, the dynamic at the company is far more productive and creative, and the people dynamics work more smoothly.

Preferences in how that appreciation is shown differ from person to person. For some, a simple thank you delivered privately to them is what they want. Even a hallway conversation or ad hoc DM where you take a moment to say, "Thank you, I noticed that," or "Great work on that project. I can see that your strengths are XYZ." Others like a more public thank you at the team meeting.

Be aware of those differences. People who don't like "public" recognition often have deep issues with their self-worth. I'm not saying they should become comfortable with celebrity-level visibility. I'm just saying to notice the people who stand in the shadows and be willing to coach them into greater inner confidence.

Ironically, the people who love public appreciation can also have deep issues with self-worth. They just manifest differently, where they require others to validate them. Be willing to notice and coach them as well. The more each person develops their self-confidence, the more the team can authentically function with high performance.

There are two pieces to the last element of motivation that I'll share here. The first piece is that **all** are motivated by understanding the purpose or reason for the change. It's why answering the question *why* is so critical—because we never stop wanting the answer to that question, even though we may have stopped directly asking the question as we got older.

As the executive leader, you need to be willing to answer that question for your team, which means you need to have dug deep enough to have an answer you can articulate beyond some parental response like "Because I said so." No one likes that. Not even you. Yes, there will be times when decisions will be made, and not everyone agrees, but everyone needs to get on board to implement them anyway. (This is why an entire chapter is devoted to creating daily habits that create teamwork, and another chapter is devoted to optimizing communication.) Being willing to be up front with answering why, and to be questioned about why later, is an essential leadership ability that raises the performance of your team.

The second piece is that **all** are motivated by understanding how their role fits into creating that change, goal, or result. Employees who seek development to raise their performance and have integrity to produce quality work always want to know how their work contributes to the big picture of the company. They want to know how what they do matters to the business and, frankly, to you, the executive leader. This is where appreciation connects with the answer to "Why?" It also connects to mapping how each person contributes to the goals of the business. Your leadership team should already know how their department and their role as a leader contribute to the bigger picture. If they don't, start there. In fact, start there anyway.

Whenever I begin working with a team, one of the first steps is to have each person present about their role on the team. Why, you ask? (See what I did there?) Because it strategically expands the business knowledge within the team, gives the person presenting an opportunity to synthesize what they do in their own mind, and creates an avenue to clarify how their work contributes to the business. Others will hear where their work falls in the processes, workflow, or client contribution, and identify the interdependencies among teams.

It also begins the process of opening the communication channels between leaders and softens any hesitation in approaching each other. This exercise is always eye-opening. "So much more than meets the eye," "I had no idea you were dealing with all of that," or "I hadn't thought about it that way" are the most common responses. My favorite is when you can see that open-mouthed look of realization that the other people are not trying to make your job harder—they have plenty of their own stuff to navigate. A few tweaks may be all it takes to make things easier.

Teamwork Tools to Activate Change

Adapting to Changing Expectations
If the business priorities are changing, look into the adaptability of your teams and the resources they need to change on a dime again. But first, double-check yourself. Is what you are changing aligned with the goals of the business, or is it just a distraction consuming everyone's time?

A Commitment to Completion
When people get confused about priorities or don't have the information they need to make good decisions, sometimes the work just stops. Ensure the completion by talking with your teams about the importance of asking for the information they need. Establish a team dynamic that embraces those questions. Better yet, create an environment for your team to function where the information is proactively shared, and people don't have to hunt for it.

The Trust and Safety to Question Each Other in Times of High Stress
How the team functions in stress is truly a test of the degree of teamwork. Do they pull together, stop, run to someone else, or trust each other to figure out a solution? See the T.R.U.S.T. Model in Chapter 5.

Accept That Mistakes Will Happen
Periods of change always raise the risk of mistakes. Regardless of how much development and training people have received, mistakes will still happen. We're all still human. The pivot point is what happens when there is a mistake. Do people take it in stride and determine what to do next, or do they freak out in blame and shame?

Pause and Calmly Navigate the Unexpected
Huddling together is a great response to the unexpected. Not to gossip

about it but to address the situation--what's known, what isn't, what can be controlled, what can't, and what more information is needed to make good decisions. Sometimes, the information you want isn't available, so then the next question is: What quality of decision can you make based on what you know now? What is the risk for each option? Then, make the choice and move forward.

Conversation—and More Conversation

I've heard some clients express frustration with "overcommunication." Other clients state, "You can never have enough communication." As you might imagine, I'm in the second camp. More conversation is better than less. Learn the ways to make it more streamlined, and those of you who think "overcommunication" is a thing will feel less so.

Sticky Situations

Handling Work Breakdowns and People Conflicts

Someone forgot to do something. They knew about it. They had intended to do it. They got distracted, and it didn't happen. If it only affected one person, the one who forgot, that would be awesome, wouldn't it? Rarely does one person's breakdown only impact them. Now you have some conflict because the person who is responsible for the next step in the process or project cannot do it because someone messed up.

Is there compassion for the person who messed up? Or just blame? Is there lasting anger and frustration, or does the team move right into problem-solving? Does the person who messed up feel remorseful and apologize, or do they just act like nothing is wrong? These are all indications of how your team is functioning, and each of these dynamics impacts the productivity of *everyone* on the team, regardless of whether they were directly involved in the situation or not.

Activating change sometimes takes the form of handling situations in the moment. How you lead yourself and your team through a situation where someone messed up shows how you lead. It also demonstrates how you absorb mistakes, pivot, adjust, and move forward. If your team can productively do this without your intervention, you're on the road of healthy team dynamics.

Time to Strategically Think, Consider, and Explore

In times of intense change, time is always of the essence. It's like we forgot that we still have the same number of hours in a day that we did last week. It's easy to get pulled into leading in a rush on autopilot. This is where the *lead* part of Lead Not React™ from Chapter 4 shows up yet again. Even if it's a fire that just started today, give yourself time to pause and consider the whole picture.

Depending upon what's changing, it's critical that you, the leader, invest the time to consider the immediate and longer-term impact of the choices that are made. Remember that your teams are counting on you to have the strategic viewpoint and to embrace their input to deepen your understanding of the impact.

Now that we've discussed all *5 Pivotal Growth Principles*, let's explore how they make leading easier by triggering the right chain reaction for growth. I'll set you up for success in the next chapter.

CHAPTER 9

THE CHAIN REACTION FOR DELIBERATE GROWTH®

*When you harness business momentum,
you now have growth power.*

Y OU CREATE GROWTH. YEP, YOU, THE LEADER, CREATE GROWTH BY leading, not reacting, and by transforming blind spots, actively creating teamwork each day, and clarifying your vision, direction, and expectations. You create growth when the goals are mutually understood, and everyone in your company has two-way conversations with each other so that the effort made to implement growth is spent on things that create the right chain reaction for growth. Remember my client who wanted to raise revenue but mapped the action plan to decrease expenses? Managing expenses is a good thing to do, but it won't raise revenue. That was not the right chain reaction for their growth goals.

The Bottom Line: What Chain Reaction Means

The numbers on your financial statements were created by someone who did something or didn't do something. Someone who made a decision or didn't make a decision, which is actually a decision. Someone who was thinking something through or jumping to conclusions and guessing. Someone who had the information they needed or made assumptions and hoped. Every single piece of financial information and result was created by humans. Every. Single. Piece.

Some of you might be thinking that piece of capital equipment that shows up on your balance sheet had nothing to do with a human. It was a number entered into the financial system. Well, someone entered the number, and someone researched that equipment and decided to buy it. Someone made the business case to buy it and determined that there was budget for it. That information came from either you, your leadership team, or someone inside the business. So, that seemingly innocuous financial number on a statement that represents a piece of equipment still came from a human who did or didn't do something inside your organization.

This is what I mean by chain reaction. **People** create it.

The chain reaction that creates growth is created by the people. As I've said throughout this book, it's the decisions that are made every day in every text, in every email, in every hallway conversation, every DM chat, every in-person or virtual meeting, and every phone call.

What are those decisions based on???

Answering that question is the key to knowing how to create the right chain reaction that builds growth instead of confusion, and builds expansion instead of expensive rework. That creates the path where you will actually have the results you seek. That values the people who used their time and energy in their careers at your company to collectively build your mission together.

When motivated leaders understand how to make and lead better decisions, they activate the right chain reaction for Deliberate Growth®.

Set Up Conditions for Success

The *5 Pivotal Principles for Leading Deliberate Growth*® are designed to create the right chain reaction. If you want to leverage your time, energy, and money and create effective *and* efficient growth, <u>always begin with the first one</u>, *Lead Not React*™, and proceed in order. As I developed these transformational elements throughout my thirty-year career and used them with clients, leaders have experienced how all five integrate together.

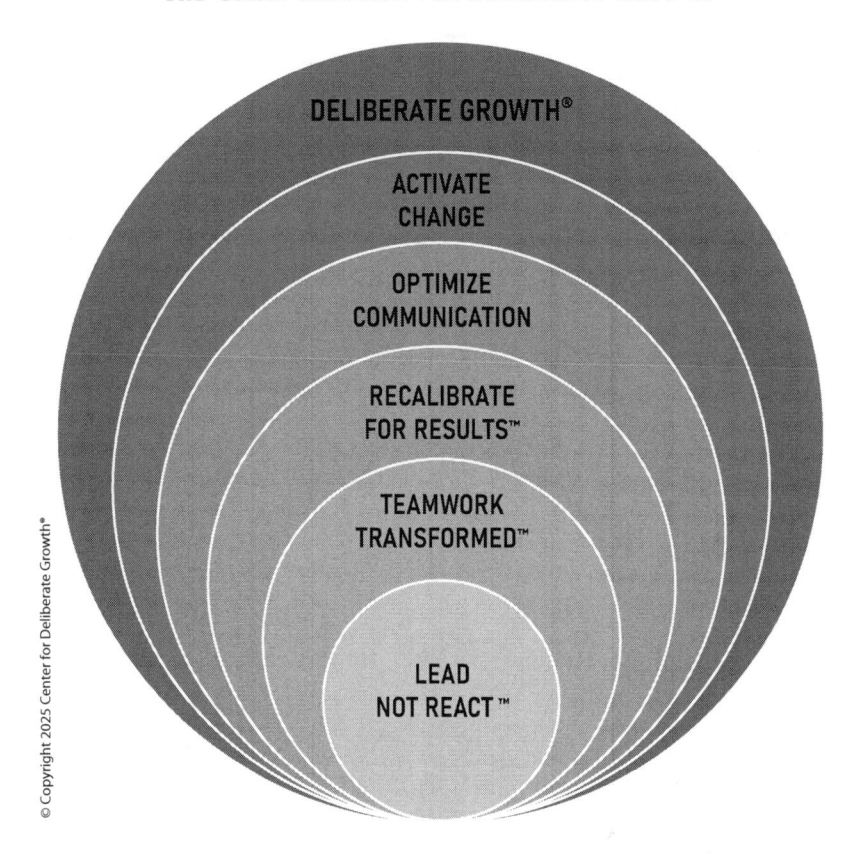

The 5 Pivotal Principles for Leading Deliberate Growth®

Pivotal Growth Principle #1: Lead Not React™
First, get your head on straight. Because *you are always leading*, develop your Growth Mindset and emotional intelligence (often referred to as EQ). This is embracing the need to understand your own emotions and those of others. Are you leading deliberately or by default, aka on autopilot? You want to understand yourself well enough to recognize if you are operating from a Growth Mindset or a Fixed Mindset. Functioning with Empowering Beliefs about people, the situation, and yourself puts you in a Growth Mindset. If Limiting Beliefs sneak in, you've slipped into a Fixed Mindset and are probably jumping to conclusions. It's okay if that happens; we're all human. The question is: Do you notice when it

happens and embrace being questioned? This is key to being approachable, to understand your own blind spots, and for your team to want to follow you.

Pivotal Growth Principle #2: Teamwork Transformed™

Make teamwork a verb so it's a daily activity. Because trust is the foundation of any relationship, I've found it can be easier to develop when you understand what builds it. (See my T.R.U.S.T. Builds Teamwork Model in Chapter 5 for an overview of the components.) Ensure that your people feel valued. Are your teams comfortable speaking up with ideas and issues or when they make mistakes? Are they comfortable asking questions and being questioned? Everyone on the team has a role in creating growth. Every. Person. Ensure that each person understands their role and how it contributes to the success of the growth. And the impact on the business and their teammates when they do something that interferes with it. *Commit* to teamwork.

Pivotal Growth Principle #3: Recalibrate for Results™

Is there *alignment* among the purpose of the growth, the resulting priorities, the people who need to be part of implementing it, and the business results it will create? The action plan and effort required to create the growth must be matched to the desired outcome. It sounds obvious, but it's easy to overlook this part. Handoffs of information or projects between teams are a frequent risk point for decreased productivity. Understand how your role as the executive leader can make or break the alignment, along with your teams' understanding of the interdependent nature of how they function within the organization.

Pivotal Growth Principle #4: Optimize Communication

Better communication is hands down the fastest way to improve efficiency in how you function as a business. How information flows through the organization is based on the communication channels and methods that are part of your culture. Develop the communication skills needed in you and your team(s) to close the gaps in your abilities. Use the *3C Core Communication Model* to structure the conversation and create mutual understanding. Assess whether you are maximizing the *Automatic Avenues of Accountability* using facilitation and listening skills. Don't assume that communication will take care of itself. It requires its own plan for the alignment in the prior principle to become a reality. Your Growth Mindset about communication manifests in healthy team dynamics, productive teamwork, alignment, and change being possible.

Pivotal Growth Principle #5: Activate Change

Are you waiting for something bad to happen and hoping it doesn't? Are you anticipating merely "making it through?" Instead, be prepared to proactively create change by leveraging the *5 Factors for Leading Change*. Understand what it takes to motivate and manage proactive change. Assess what external events that you cannot control are infiltrating or stopping your decisions. Have someone to lead the changes required for growth. It might be you. It might be someone else. You might have a blind spot about activating change (or any of the *Pivotal Growth Principles*). Seek feedback and guidance from your coach, or contact me for help.

When planning changes, companies often dissect the financial elements of creating the change and overlook the people required for it to become successful. Create an intentional plan to engage the people and show them what makes this change valuable to the business and to them.

I'll remind you again that the chain reaction for growth is created by **people**—people who are thinking from a Growth Mindset, people who are committed to teamwork, people who have built their inner confidence to be questioned and to ask questions, people who understand the alignment of goals, priorities, and actions, and people who know how to spot gaps.

Interdependent Decisions

Wherever you are starting from today, the growth you seek will happen when you begin to understand what *allows* it to happen and what *interferes* with it happening.

With the integration of all *5 Pivotal Principles for Leading Deliberate Growth®*, it's time to dig deeper into becoming more strategic in your decision-making. As you develop self-awareness in your mindset and leadership style, and recognize how that impacts your teams' performance, you're seeing the interdependencies between how you lead and how your teams perform. This means you are realizing that there's a chain reaction that happens when someone makes a decision and another chain reaction as a result of that decision, creating interdependences between each decision and each person who makes one. Yikes!

I've said before that everyone in the business makes decisions, not just the "decision-makers." I've also said that each person makes decisions every time they do something or don't do something or prioritize something or don't prioritize something: answer the phone, return a call, or make time to help a teammate. The question continues—what are those decisions based on???

Before and After

When you embrace my *5 Pivotal Principles for Leading Deliberate Growth®*, people's decisions are based on their own expertise and knowledge plus real, aligned information from within the business; communication is optimized, and change is mobilized.

Leadership Decisions <u>Before</u> the 5 Pivotal Principles for Leading Deliberate Growth®

DECISION GAP	DECISION AREA	DECISION BLIND SPOT
Most Often Skipped	Lack of focus on the future	Get through right now. There isn't time or money to consider anything else anyway.
Most Overlooked	Impact on your teams	They will figure it out after I decide.
Most Misunderstood	How to best follow through	It won't be that complicated, although I didn't ask anyone for their input.
Most Often Missing	Planning communication	I already said it once, even though what I know has changed since then; I'm not going to repeat myself.
Most Overwhelming	Just "getting through" change	Hunker down and hope it's over soon and that we survive.

© Copyright 2025 Center for Deliberate Growth®

Leadership Decisions <u>After</u> the 5 Pivotal Principles for Leading Deliberate Growth®

DECISION ATTITUDE	DECISION AREA	DECISIONS TO LEAD DELIBERATE GROWTH®
Knowing Where to Start	What are we really trying to accomplish? WHY that?	Navigate problems and possibilities through a Growth Mindset. Connect to the purpose of the business, project, or issue.
Being Effective	How do we best implement and follow through?	Goals filter decisions about priorities and action steps. Stakeholders are identified and included appropriately.
Impacting People	What development and resources do your teams need? What do you need?	Developing teamwork expands ideas and aids planning. Valuing each team member deepens engagement, builds employee satisfaction, and raises productivity.
Building Efficiency	Who needs what information to make sound decisions?	Leverage everyone's time and prevent the cost of rework.
Thinking Boldly Proactive	What will reduce stress and create desired results?	Map the value of the change to the executive leader(s), teams, stakeholders, and business.

© Copyright 2025 Center for Deliberate Growth®

Be careful not to assume that you can skip ahead to the "after" decision matrix without reading the chapters about the *5 Pivotal Principles for Leading Deliberate Growth®* first. It won't work like you might assume, and without the preparation, you might not recognize why. You'll just be frustrated by the inconsistent results and growing stress you see in your teams and unsure of how to change it. Perhaps how you felt when you began reading this book.

The Decision to Survive or Thrive

In working with the new CEO of a small and established construction service business, the existing priorities had distilled down to survival. But this CEO wanted to thrive, and she knew that she needed to shake things up with a different way to think about the business.

When I asked her the question, "What does the business need?" the answer was "To broaden our customer base." But in order to do that, they needed more equipment and more staff. Their current staff and equipment were maxed out. Unfortunately, that meant that the existing customers had to wait for service.

What was already in place was experienced people who could train new staff. The challenge would be to arrange the customer schedule so that the people who could teach the new hires were available.

The stakeholders were everyone in the business because everyone was stretched. The silent partner in the company was also a big stakeholder because he wasn't realizing the financial impact that he expected from the business. The business was breaking even, but it wasn't growing.

In working with me on her mindset, this CEO agreed to go talk with her team. While she knew she wanted to shake things up, she had some resistance to the idea because she *assumed* this team would be resistant. See that Limiting Belief sneaking in there and messing with her mindset?

With my coaching, she boldly forged ahead and asked them about expanding the customer base and serving their existing customers better. The CEO said, "We're going to invest in equipment to expand growth. That needs to happen, and I'm going to need your help." After they stopped groaning, they quickly started problem-solving. She was surprised.

Her team was all-in on the conversation because they'd been working ten-hour days trying to serve who they already had, plus take on new customers. The focus then became "How can we train new staff?" because that was the solution the business needed.

If I had allowed this CEO to begin with time and money, the restriction felt with those two resources never would have allowed this growth conversation to happen. It would have been over before it started, with everyone walking away and hanging their head, wondering how anything is ever going to change and concluding that nothing will because nothing is possible. This is how your team stays stuck functioning the way they are now with no hope.

Notice in this example how much *the team wanted to be part of the solution*. They wanted to be involved. So, involve them. In fact, your *engaged* teams at all levels of the company want to be involved. When I talked about the importance of answering the question "Why?" earlier in this book, I mentioned that it is the number one question that engages the team. Involving them inside the solution lets them *live that why* with you. It deepens their engagement and commitment to the organization.

The thing is . . . this company didn't need to add ten new staff, which is what people mistakenly assumed and were overwhelmed by. See what assumptions do?!? They needed to add two people. And they did. The team figured out how to balance training new staff with serving existing customers so that everyone would benefit, including them. The business grew just like the CEO intended, and they shifted from survive to thrive.

It sounds so easy when I describe it, right? Like duh . . . of course it shifted how the business functions. Yet, you know that CEO had to dig deep into some mental energy and gumption to change her own mindset, as well as that of her team. Not to mention satisfying the silent owner of the business in the process.

This is where it starts. This is where it always starts, whether you want it to or not. It starts with you, the leader. This CEO was determined to be the solution, shake up this company, and create a better life for her employees and herself, and a better experience for their customers. These are the clients who speak to my soul, and it's why I do what I do to help them.

Focused Momentum for Business Prosperity

When you use all 5 *Pivotal Principles for Leading Deliberate Growth*® and stick to them, it becomes a part of how you explore possibilities, problem-solve, and innovate. The momentum created when the organization leverages this method means you are focused on what directly relates to the goals with plenty of wiggle room to innovate new ideas. You are a less stressed-out leader because you know you have explored the angles and avenues of each choice. You've delegated work to others in the context of development, not dumping, and taught others to do the same. Regardless of how much experience you have, there's a boost to your genuine confidence in how you lead, why you lead that way, and the resulting impact.

With greater self-awareness comes a better understanding of your own emotions and how they influence your behavior and decisions as a leader. You develop an understanding of your own value, more deeply own your value, and are willing to speak up and voice your value. It's what you want for yourself and what your teams need to be engaged and productive. Interactions become more seamless with you and between your teams as you model the interactive dynamics you want to create in your company culture.

Problem-solving is more collaborative—with less contentious conflict and less time-wasting avoidance. People speak up with new ideas without fear of retribution or worry about looking stupid.

There's far more time efficiency as people are on the same page and understand how to stay there. Information flows to those who need it versus working in isolating silos or just being unaware of how their role impacts others. The *Pivotal Growth Principles* deepen the understanding of how each person's role impacts others' work productivity.

When an international technology company came to me to develop its leaders, the COO had identified a group of fifteen leadership peers. This group represented all five divisions of the company. This client's program began right before the pandemic hit, so when the lockdown started, I converted the entire program to virtual within a week. Everyone was a little apprehensive about that, including me. We were already stressed about being in a pandemic, something no one had experienced before, and now their leadership development opportunity was going to be . . . online? Yep. It was already going to be a hybrid program because some of the leaders were remote. Now, everyone was going to be a virtual participant.

The COO and I reimagined how this was going to work and serve each person, including her, especially since one of the primary objectives was to build bridges between company divisions, which was now going to be done virtually. The other objectives were to help each leader understand how to lead effectively and to address the blind spots that were interfering with their productivity and their peace.

It worked. People even made time to attend on their vacations because the sessions "were so valuable," as they told me. The COO earnestly shared one day that she gained ten times more than she invested in this program, just in her own leadership development.

I coached this group and the COO through the most relevant pieces of the *5 Pivotal Principles for Leading Deliberate Growth®* over ten months. As a result, this company saved about $200,000 in employee turnover costs and $150,000 in saved time, according to interviews with each person and the COO. These are their numbers, not mine. The *Pivotal Growth Principles* create more inner confidence for leaders and have tangible results if you choose to measure them.

In fact, two of these key leaders were retained in the business. No one knew they were at risk of leaving. They didn't really want to leave.

They had confidentially shared with me after the program that they were heading out . . . until my work with the team began, and they could see change happening. "Now I know what to do differently," they said to me. So, they stayed at the company.

Helping leaders become better leaders—those who are motivated to become better leaders—is my passion. It means that I get to help make people's lives better because I'm building leaders who transform how they lead. Those leaders develop better teams. And those teams create better businesses.

Once you create that chain reaction, how do you sustain those results? And continue the upward momentum? You made it this far—the next chapter guides you on how to keep going. Let's dive into how you can make *Leading for Deliberate Growth*® more automatic.

CHAPTER 10

THE RIPPLE EFFECT

*Daily choices become long-term decisions.
Are you being deliberate, or are you leading by default?*

WHEN YOU RECOGNIZE THAT **ALL** PEOPLE IN YOUR ORGANIZATION make decisions every moment of every day, *Leading for Deliberate Growth®* becomes more automatic. How? You've internalized how important your mindset is. Then, when you combine deeper self-awareness about your mindset and emotional intelligence (also referred to as EQ) with new knowledge about how to lead, new ways of thinking emerge. This new thinking creates new behavior, and the new behavior builds deeper impact, inside and outside the business.

Growth becomes streamlined as you continuously transform your mindset, gain necessary business knowledge, develop leadership abilities, and then consistently implement what you are learning. You're now making strategic decisions that create the right chain reaction for *Deliberate Growth®* for you, your teams, and the business. That upward momentum requires consistent attention to help ensure that you don't regress back to your old ways.

Let's contrast the ripple effects of when a leader is *Leading for Deliberate Growth®* and when the leader may be *preventing* growth. It comes down to *empowerment versus control.* For my financial executive readers, leading by control is a different kind of control than the practice of "control" in financials.

Below, I'm referring to a leader who is controlling, even micromanaging.

Leading by Control Prevents Growth

MINDSET:
COMMAND, MY WAY

- Blame
- Push Around
- Read My Mind
- Resent Mistakes
- Stuck in Old Ways

LEADING BY CONTROL

© Copyright 2025 Center for Deliberate Growth®

A controlling leader stops growth and even actively prevents it. The ripple effect of this blind spot is felt throughout your teams as they give up on being valued and secretly disengage. The good people leave, and you're stuck with the employees you'd rather not keep. Growth feels impossible because you, the leader, are trying to lead from a lone ranger island, but you cannot run the business by yourself. Still, you keep trying. So, you're working long hours, hearing complaints from your family and friends, feeling stuck just like your teams, and worrying about your health. Stop this madness!

Some of you might be thinking that you're not this much of a control freak. You do some empowering things, and you do some things that you've now learned are a bit controlling. Great! That's progress. Now dig deeper. The nuances of where you are leading by control and leading by empowerment matter. It's where the blind spots that block growth live. It's also where you transform your new self-awareness into growth for yourself, your team, and the business.

Because you are the solution, do this instead: Lead by Empowerment.

Leading by Empowerment Enables Growth

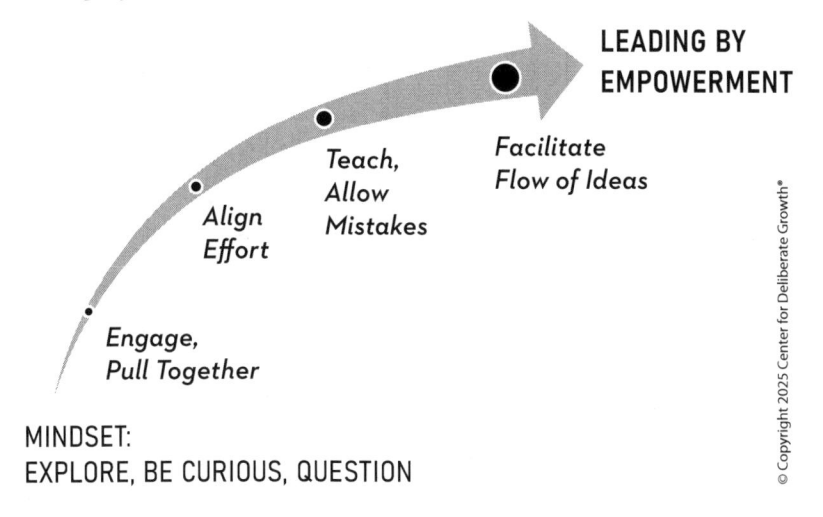

LEADING BY EMPOWERMENT

- Facilitate Flow of Ideas
- Teach, Allow Mistakes
- Align Effort
- Engage, Pull Together

MINDSET: EXPLORE, BE CURIOUS, QUESTION

© Copyright 2025 Center for Deliberate Growth®

Leading by empowerment creates growth through the right chain reaction of decisions. It begins with your Growth Mindset as you Lead Not React™ and teach your teams to do the same. When you leverage all 5 *Pivotal Principles for Leading Deliberate Growth®*, leading becomes easier. I didn't say it would be without surprises or obstacles, but in using this method, you are equipped because you know what empowers you, you know how to motivate your team, you know how to align priorities with effort, and you have discovered that you can proactively create change.

A Story of Control Versus Empowerment

One leadership team client wanted to significantly alter their organizational structure. It meant changing how the people were grouped, the teams were assigned, and who everyone reported to. Activating this kind of change is not a small undertaking, and the larger the organization, the more complex it becomes. This was an established non-profit of about five hundred employees with a long track record of traditions surrounding how they functioned. The fact that they had executive leaders who wanted to explore making changes was unheard of in the history of the organization as the legacy of leadership there was leading by control.

These outside-of-the-box leaders wanted to change everything in the organizational structure because the business had become stagnant. Things were working but not evolving, and very little innovation was happening. People didn't talk in meetings or offer ideas. The quality of their service was at risk, and leaders were frustrated by the rapidly growing problems with team performance. Very little they had tried seemed to redirect the performance.

As the grapevine got a hold of this rumor of change, there was a lot of scoffing, scowling, and stubborn "never going to participate in that crazy nonsense" energy. This was a big issue for some of the long-time employees who were accustomed to things "being a certain way." Did you hear that Fixed Mindset? The people who were newer to the business were excited that someone was finally paying attention! Hello, Growth Mindset!

As I worked with the executive leadership team about their own mindset, they had many "Aha!" moments when it came to how their leadership style impacted the lack of energy and performance in their teams. That was a little rough for them as they realized that they were part of the problem. It really stung when they figured out the way they wanted to change the organization was still leading by control, even though it appeared like they were making good changes. The perplexed looks on their faces were quite normal. I see that in every client at some point. The question became, "What is the real purpose of these changes?"

As we dug deeper into the *why* of this reorg, the leaders realized they initially had a mindset of asking me to "fix everyone else" and transformed their thinking to "help all of us!"—including the executive team. They still wanted to reorganize the internal structure, though they now understood that the reasons included many more dimensions than "forcing" the employees to work differently as a result of the reorg.

Now, the reasons for the reorg were legitimately going to change the productivity of the teams. How? The executive leaders now understood that information flow is the key outcome of better communication, which meant that the delivery of services was going to become far more efficient in ways they hadn't ever considered.

This essential "Aha!" moment about the ripple effect of their decisions opened their minds to how making these complex changes was going to help their services grow. When we first met, their mindset was stuck in managing the problems they were seeing, and this reorg was, in their minds, the solution to those problems. Here we are again at strategic thinking or lack thereof. They admitted to being stuck in the weeds, which is one of the reasons they asked for my coaching. I facilitated the flow of ideas on their behalf. It's really difficult to see all the angles when you are neck-deep in the situation. I am a coach, and, again, I have a coach for this very reason because I'm still a human with blind spots.

So, what happened? We mapped the emerging alignment this reorg would create and then explored the resulting changes in leadership and the reporting structure. I coached these executives to lead by example and work with their leaders in empowering new ways. It gave everyone permission to do things differently. These leaders thanked me for "keeping them on the road and moving ahead," because otherwise they were "headed for the ditch."

It turned out there were more people secretly wishing someone would rip out the "old ways of doing things" than anticipated. The more the changes happened, the more growth started to accelerate as the teams became more engaged in the process. Yes, there were still the hecklers and naysayers. We are talking about humans here. But in this new way of leading, the hecklers didn't rule how the organization functioned anymore. These leaders were no longer tolerant of that Fixed Mindset and its accompanying attitude. Even peer pressure among the teams to "change and grow" meant those who were stuck either needed to ask for help or work elsewhere. Both events happened.

Some of you are cheering right now because you've experienced the relief when "bad apples" leave the business. If you're the leader reading this, and you're worried about the turnover this caused, notice your mindset about that. Notice the Limiting Beliefs about fearing employee turnover. Yes, it's a pain in the neck when it's someone you really want to keep. In this situation, however, we're talking about people actively resisting evolution in the organization and stubbornly being roadblocks. Those aren't really the people you want to keep, right? Yes, if they are a subject matter expert, that will sting if they leave. Yet, your stress could quickly go down because their negative mindset and its ripple effect left with them. Your teams will also breathe a sigh of relief.

The Keys to Leading Deliberate Growth®

Those out-of-the-box thinking leaders embraced these keys to leading *Deliberate Growth®* for themselves, the teams, and the organization. Use these to create ongoing forward momentum.

Pivotal Growth Principle #1: Lead Not React™

- Mindset is the root of effective leadership. How you think about people, the problem or opportunity, and yourself is the beginning of whether you are solving something or making it worse. Are you using a leader's mindset or operating on autopilot?
- Decisions are made every day in every interaction by every person across the business, not just "decision-makers." What are they based on?
- Strategic thinking means stepping back to look at the whole situation or scenario. Look across the organization, not in silos.
- Emotional intelligence is the biggest gap in mindset that impacts a leader's style, influence, and effectiveness. Build your internal emotional intelligence and learn how to use it with others.
- Delegate means develop, not dump.

Pivotal Growth Principle #2: Teamwork Transformed™

- *Commit* to teamwork.
- Teamwork is a verb and requires daily attention to engage your team.
- Build teamwork through T.R.U.S.T.
- This is where the collaboration you seek lives. It's also what makes advanced problem-solving easier and faster.
- Leading by example *shows* your teams how you want to be approached and how you want people to interact with each other.
- Be willing to get out of your comfort zone, be uncomfortable, and be coachable to learn new ways of leading. Your leadership abilities are visible to your teams, the board, the bank, suppliers, investors, owners, vendors, partners, stockholders, clients/customers, and other stakeholders.

Pivotal Growth Principle #3: Recalibrate for Results™

- If your business priorities and people's actions are not aligned with the goal, you'll go in circles instead of grow. This sounds simple, but it isn't. This sounds obvious, yet I see gaps in alignment with every client.
- Use the goal as the filter for decisions. Otherwise, alignment won't happen, and effort will be wasted.
- Be aware of the "cool factor" distracting you from what will actually create results. Some of you would call this scope creep. Others would say this is the stuff that you could do for your client or customer, but they didn't ask for it. Now, decide if it's a critical factor or just a distraction costing you time and potentially money.

- Competing priorities will always be an issue. Learn to decipher what directly impacts the goals. This concretely impacts capacity planning, yours as the executive leader and each of your team's.
- Intentional alignment maximizes results and minimizes the risk of rework. Do the steps to design alignment in order.

Pivotal Growth Principle #4: Optimize Communication

- Better communication is the fastest way to raise efficiency in a business because it's really about information flow.
- Improving communication is the output of changing other things like mindset, attitude about interactions, self-awareness, and developing new skills.
- Ask more questions. Assume less and ask for information.
- Listening is the most underused communication skill, yet it has the most impact on creating mutual understanding the first time.
- The cost of rework is preventable. The solution to rework lands in the leadership mindset and communication skills of the leader first, and the entire organization second. Every person contributes to creating rework or preventing it.
- Meetings are one of the most effective and efficient methods of communication and information flow. Learn what it takes to facilitate them well.

Pivotal Growth Principle #5: Activate Change

- Decide to create change instead of waiting for it to happen to you or constantly trying to catch up to it. Here we are back to mindset.

- Develop business and industry knowledge. This is the technical knowledge required for each person to do their job well, including you, the executive leader. It directly impacts the quality of decisions that are made by each person and the pace at which change can be implemented. Prioritize training to ensure there are no gaps in technical knowledge.
- Leverage the five factors to lead change.
- Invest in coaching to ensure leadership abilities are developed in each person.

Success Factors

As the leader, *it turns out being the problem and the solution is a good thing.* Because you have absolute choice over which path to take for yourself, and which path you will create for your team, to maximize the ripple effect of growth in the business.

What does it take? It takes:

- Self-leadership, confidence, and courage.
- Being willing to step outside your comfort zone; develop your growth edges to expand or improve your leadership abilities.
- Being open to thinking differently and doing things differently.
- Being coachable.
- Self-awareness of assumptions/bias.
- Head plus heart decision-making and strategic thinking.
- Exploring blind spots and power blocks.
- Collaboration and teamwork.
- Clarity of direction and a shared purpose with your team.
- Communication flow.
- Consistent use of Automatic Avenues of Accountability.
- Measuring activities that create progress, not perfection, and using KPIs to measure what moves you, your team, and the business forward.

- Leading change.
- Asking more questions.
- A "lesson learned" attitude instead of thinking everything is a big failure.

An important note: **everyone** uses leadership skills and abilities, not just you and your other leaders. **All** employees have a job to do, and part of becoming a more effective person is by leading yourself. The *Pivotal Growth Principles* outlined in this book help all of us to do that for ourselves and with each other. Get started. (The first step might be to contact Debra!)

What's Possible Now?

When you leverage all 5 *Pivotal Principles for Leading Deliberate Growth*®, everyone is making decisions based on real information that each person needs to be effective in their roles and in their teams.

> ***Learning to be intentional about your thought process as a leader, and creating an active team dynamic, means sustainable business results with less effort.***

As a result . . .

- There's ease and flow to your days instead of chaos and turmoil as you understand your own mindset and power blocks.
- Even if the unexpected happens or something starts burning—putting out the fire feels easier as you work together to determine a solution.
- You notice more efficiency because of fewer assumptions and more purposeful conversations.
- Advanced problem-solving gets smoother as people are open to learning about new blind spots and doing things differently.

- Better decisions mean more efficient *and* effective actions.
- Interactive dynamics within teams are easier and more vibrant.
- Handoffs between teams are more efficient and effective without fear of conflict and pointing fingers as people focus on the goal of the project and how they all contribute to creating it.
- Accountability happens without you.
- Ownership of responsibilities lives in each person.
- Innovation in products, processes, or *that person*'s specific responsibilities is easily voiced.

The business thrives because everyone knows *why* they work there and *how* their work contributes to the organization's success.

Let's Connect.
In my experience coaching executive leaders, they feel a deep sense of relief when they finally have an ally who tells the absolute truth. Maybe you have a business partner who does this, or maybe you have a peer group in the company. If you don't have either, how would it feel to have an expert to learn from or bounce ideas off of to deepen your self-awareness, examine issues, or explore opportunities?

After reading through all of the *Pivotal Growth Principles*, you might be feeling apprehensive about how to get started, or maybe you identified how you want to proceed from here. Wherever your mindset is right now, it's a good place to begin.

Let's revitalize how you think about yourself as a leader to adjust how you lead. Expand your self-awareness to empower your leadership style and then experience the resulting impact on the outcomes you create with your team and grow the business.

We spend the majority of our time at work. My mission is to build better leaders who create conditions and environments where everyone thrives, including the leader. These should be places and people who empower us, develop us, and expand our potential, all while creating great business results. I choose to focus on leaders because of your influence in the lives of others, which extends my mission of developing better leaders and your mission to become a better leader more quickly.

Let's explore what's on your mind right now so we can create **Deliberate Growth**® together.

Visit *debrakunz.com* to learn more.

ACKNOWLEDGMENTS

Thank you to all my clients for their vulnerability and their trust. It's an honor to coach you to greater self-awareness through astounding opportunities, difficult challenges, and leading your teams into higher-performing dynamics. I appreciate your commitment to your own learning and making better businesses for yourself and your people.

Thank you to everyone who has been and continues to be part of my lived experience and accumulated knowledge about life and leadership.

Thank you to my fellow coaches and transformational friends Wise Hearts, BeMyBest, Pods, and BA group for your ongoing support.

Thank you to the coaches I've worked with for my own growth and development as an executive coach and entrepreneur.

Thank you to all the test readers for your thoughtful feedback.

Thank you to all my friends and family who have listened to me and cheered me on. Thank you, Mom, for inspiring me to become an author and for your editing from heaven.

ABOUT THE AUTHOR

Award-Winning Executive Coach and Author Debra Kunz has guided countless leaders toward Deliberate Growth®, empowering them with tools to achieve sustainable success. With three decades of coaching and leading through complex business challenges—including ten mergers in ten years—Debra brings a blend of practical wisdom and warm wit to her work. Recognized for her expertise in developing self-awareness and leadership strategies, Debra has developed principles that work across startups, small businesses, and large corporations. She lives in the Kansas City area and loves that she can wear the same team colors to support two of her favorites, the Kansas City Chiefs and Iowa State Cyclones.

To learn more about the author, please visit
debrakunz.com

To contact the author regarding speaking engagements,
please go to *debrakunz.com*

For all media inquiries or other questions, please go to
debrakunz.com

Made in the USA
Monee, IL
21 March 2025